Reading
and
Writing
in
Science

MARIA C. GRANT   DOUGLAS FISHER

Reading
and
Writing
in
Science

TOOLS TO DEVELOP DISCIPLINARY LITERACY

This Book Belongs to
Maurita Aubrey

CORWIN
A SAGE Company

For information:

Corwin
A SAGE Company
2455 Teller Road
Thousand Oaks, California 91320
(800) 233-9936
Fax: (800) 417-2466
www.corwinpress.com

SAGE Ltd.
1 Oliver's Yard
55 City Road
London EC1Y 1SP
United Kingdom

SAGE India Pvt. Ltd.
B 1/I 1 Mohan Cooperative
   Industrial Area
Mathura Road, New Delhi 110 044
India

SAGE Asia-Pacific Pte. Ltd.
33 Pekin Street #02-01
Far East Square
Singapore 048763

Printed in the United States of America

Library of Congress Cataloging-in-Publication Data

Grant, Maria C.
Reading and writing in science : tools to develop disciplinary literacy / Maria C. Grant, Douglas Fisher.
    p. cm.
Includes bibliographical references and index.
ISBN 978-1-4129-5613-0 (cloth)
ISBN 978-1-4129-5614-7 (pbk.)
    1. Science—Study and teaching (Secondary) 2. Science—Terminology—Study and teaching (Secondary) 3.   Language arts—Correlation with content subjects. I. Fisher, Douglas, 1965- II. Title.

Q181.G536 2010
507.1′2—dc22   2009019906

This book is printed on acid-free paper.

11 12 13 14 15 10 9 8 7 6 5 4 3 2

Acquisitions Editor:	Cathy Hernandez
Editorial Assistant:	Sarah Bartlett
Production Editor:	Amy Schroller
Copy Editor:	Tina Hardy
Typesetter:	C&M Digitals (P) Ltd.
Proofreader:	Charlotte J. Waisner
Indexer:	Judy Hunt
Cover Designer:	Michael Dubowe

Contents

Preface

This book is about teaching content literacy. More specifically, it is about teaching *science* content literacy, a realm of instruction that has sometimes been neglected by educators who place all focus on science content instruction. While we realize that it is indeed necessary to emphasize an understanding of content, we strongly feel that a focus on the specific literacy requirements of those who read, write, and talk about science is of equal import and a perfect companion to content instruction. Does this mean that we think all citizens should have some degree of science literacy? Absolutely! Consider the fact that the November 2008 elections had several key environmental initiatives for voters across the country to weigh in on. In Missouri, the voters had to decide about Proposition C, The Missouri Clean Energy Initiative, which would require the state's investor-owned electric utilities to generate or purchase two % of their electricity from renewable sources (wind, solar, biomass—including ethanol and hydropower) by the year 2011. The standard would gradually increase to 15 % by 2021. Coloradoans decided on the fate of Amendment 58, an initiative to remove a tax credit for oil and gas producers. The revenue would instead be allocated for a few select social and environmental purposes. Minnesota and California had similar environmental issues to consider as well. To be a well-informed voter, one must be able to read about an issue. Occasionally, a voter may even be called on to either write about or deliberate on the pros and cons as well. It is likely that science-related issues will continue to take the stage at election time and will often be the central focus of community forums. Today, there are citizens across the country debating issues related to drought (California has been facing this dilemma for years now), water and land pollution, ocean dumping, and environmental waste and disposal.

These are just a few of the concerns of people across the globe. It is everyday citizens, including the young people sitting in our classrooms, who have the right and the responsibility to help make these critical decisions today and well into the future. Given this, science educators can do a great service by helping their students learn to access science content in a way that fosters discussion, reflection, and authorship. Additionally, it's important to keep in mind that students who can read, write, and talk about science can go beyond the content presented in earth science or biology class. They are better able to pick up and read a newspaper article about the eruption of a Columbian volcano or contribute to a conversation about genetic engineering in an informed, knowledgeable way. Science literacy goes beyond the instruction of content. It enables students to continue to learn, reflect, and communicate about science issues throughout their lives. And clearly, science will continue to dominate our realm of existence in increasingly more powerful ways over the coming years.

As a way to frame science literacy instruction, we have considered Shanahan and Shanahan's (2008) model of literacy progression. This model views content literacy as a pinnacle sitting on top of a base that includes basic and intermediate literacy skills. Science content literacy, a specific type of disciplinary literacy, requires that a reader view a text from a framework that allows for predictions, questioning that goes beyond the text, and the possibility of experimentation. It requires readers to access background knowledge and to look for data and conclusions. Typically, science readers will move back and forth between text and charts or graphs, paying specific attention to trends and patterns. This specific lens of viewing and responding makes a science reader and science writer different from a history or English language arts reader or writer. It is what has inspired the authorship of this book. You'll notice that there are margin notes designed to clue you in to the aspects of disciplinary literacy that are central to the chapters. Additionally, you'll find a progression in the chapter sequence that will allow the reader to focus on what's important to think about at the start (Chapter 1—"The Role of Language in Science" and Chapter 2—"Developing and Activating Background Knowledge"), what's important to think about in terms of instruction (Chapter 3—"Integrating Vocabulary Instruction Into the Science Classroom," Chapter 4—"Reading Science Texts," and Chapter 5—"Writing In Science: Scaffolding Skills For Science Students"), and what's critical to an understanding of student learning and teacher instruction (Chapter 6—"Assessing Student Learning in Science").

Because this book is intended for secondary teachers—middle school, junior high, and high school educators who teach a variety of science classes—we have provided examples of instructional tools from both the physical and biological fields. Chapter 1, "The Role of Language in Science," discusses the importance of disciplinary literacy in science education and lays the foundation for an understanding of how to provide discipline-specific literacy instruction. Chapter 2, "Developing and Activating Background Knowledge," provides ways to help students build the needed background knowledge so that they can tackle an article about the quest to develop new antibiotics or listen to a podcast about cholesterol levels in children. We believe that reading in science often needs to rest on a certain amount of foundational stored information.

In addition to background knowledge, science readers need to have a solid store of technical and academic words, along with the skills to decipher or predict unknown, new terms. That's what Chapter 3, "Integrating Vocabulary Instruction Into the Science Classroom," is all about. Chapter 4, "Reading Science Texts," explores the ways in which readers in the discipline of science approach texts. This chapter includes strategies for comprehension, ways to guide and build science reading skills while simultaneously accessing content, and ideas for releasing the responsibility of learning to students. Chapter 5, "Writing in Science: Scaffolding Skills for Science Students," provides ways to get students started on science writing, including the use of writing frames, graphic organizers, writing-to-learn, and a writing protocol. Finally, Chapter 6, "Assessing Student Learning in Science," discusses the use of formative assessment, including how it can be used to both improve instruction and target specific needs of students. There is also a section in this chapter on creating purposeful assessments.

We are hopeful that this book will get you thinking about the various ways that students can learn from science texts so that they are better able to reflect on content, generate new ideas, and share content-based thoughts. While we bring in research-based theory and instructional ideas, we intend for this to be a jumping-off point for our reader educators. We provide a way to approach science literacy with a discipline-specific lens, but we intend for our readers to build on this so that individual science students, each unique in concerns and interests, in classrooms around the globe, can learn about, think about, and write about science that is relevant to them in their own corners of the world.

Acknowledgments

Corwin gratefully acknowledges the contributions of the following reviewers:

Trina Allen
Science Content Specialist
Research and Development,
  Measurement Incorporated
Durham, NC

C. Elise Barrett
Assistant Clinical Professor of
  Education
The University of North
  Carolina–Chapel Hill
Chapel Hill, NC

Regina Brinker
Science Teacher
Christensen Middle School
Livermore, CA

Diane Callahan
Science Teacher
Fairfield Middle School
West Chester, OH

Kelly Deters
Science Teacher
Shawnee Heights High School
Tecumseh, KS

Jeremy Dove
Science Teacher/Curriculum
  Advisor
Monticello High School
Charlottesville, VA

Zoe Evans
Seventh-Grade Science Teacher
Central Middle School
Carrollton, GA

Kathy Ferrell
Instructional Coach
Excelsior Springs Middle School
Excelsior Springs, MO

Debra Greenstone
Science Teacher
Mount Pleasant High School
Wilmington, DE

Christopher Harris
Assistant Professor, College of
  Education
University of Arizona
Tucson, AZ

Jane Hunn
Eighth-Grade Science Teacher
Tippecanoe Valley Middle School
Akron, IN

Susan Leeds
Science Department Chair and
    Gifted Studies
Howard Middle School
Winter Park, FL

Mark Little
AP Biology and Anatomy Teacher
Broomfield High School
Broomfield, CO

Kristin T. Rearden
Clinical Associate Professor of
    Science Education
University of Tennessee
Knoxville, TN

Charre Todd
Science Teacher
Norman Middle School
Crossett, AR

Rick Walton
Eighth-Grade Earth Science
    Teacher
Eastern Heights Middle School
Elyria, OH

Randy Yerrick
Professor of Science Education
San Diego State University
San Diego, CA

About the Authors

Maria Grant, EdD, is Associate Professor in the Department of Secondary Education at California State University, Fullerton and a classroom teacher at Health Sciences High & Middle College. She works with both preservice and veteran teachers in the credential and graduate programs. Her work includes research and publications in the area of literacy integration into content areas, with a central focus on science education. In addition to her efforts at the university, Dr. Grant's experience includes over 19 years of teaching in high school science classrooms. She has taught physics, oceanography, coordinated science, chemistry, and earth science. Additionally, she has acted as a leader in curriculum development and professional development at both the school and district levels. Her current efforts include professional development work centered on formative assessment. She can be reached at mgrant@fullerton.edu.

Douglas Fisher, PhD, is Professor of Language and Literacy Education in the Department of Teacher Education at San Diego State University and a classroom teacher at Health Sciences High & Middle College. He is the recipient of an International Reading Association Celebrate Literacy Award, the Farmer award for excellence in writing from the National Council of Teachers of English, as well as a Christa McAuliffe award for excellence in teacher education. He has published numerous articles on reading and literacy, differentiated instruction, and curriculum design as well as books, such as *Creating Literacy-Rich Schools for Adolescents* (with Gay Ivey), *Checking for Understanding: Formative Assessments for Your Classroom* (with Nancy Frey), *Better Learning Through Structured Teaching* (with Nancy Frey), and *Content-Area Conversations: How to Plan Discussion-Based Lessons for Diverse Learners* (with Carol Rothenberg). He can be reached at dfisher@mail.sdsu.edu.

We would like to acknowledge the wonderful students and teachers at Health Sciences High and Middle College for helping us to deepen our understanding of how teaching and learning are so intimately connected.

This book is dedicated to the best family in the universe—George, Ruth Mary, Nathaniel, Christen, Moriah, David, and Ruthie—with love.

The Role of Language in Science   1

Teaching science is exciting. Sharing the biological, physical, and social world with students is a wonderful experience. Students love to learn about themselves and their world and are often thrilled with lab experiences and other hands-on learning opportunities provided to them in the science classroom.

A look inside a classroom confirms this. Andrew sits excitedly at a lab bench. His class has been studying human systems, and they've finally gotten to the nervous system, which Andrew has been waiting for all year. His biology teacher has told the students that they get to dissect sheep brains and examine the structures of the sheep's central nervous system.

Andrew and his lab partners glove up, ready to begin. They weigh the brain and then they separate the two hemispheres and measure them. They find the corpus callosum and then begin labeling the lobes. They find the cranial nerves. The lab progresses for several days while students investigate the structures in the sheep brain. Andrew is in heaven. He loves this work and can't wait to get back to class each day.

Labs are exciting and powerful ways for students to learn science. However, our purpose here is not to provide science lab instruction. There are a number of excellent resources available related to designing science labs (e.g., Shevick, 1998). But in this book, we want to explore the reading and writing components of science that prepare students for the inquiry work they do in labs.

In the case of Andrew's very exciting experience, his teacher did a significant amount of work so that students would be prepared for the lab. Andrew's teacher, Mr. Jeffers, read to the class daily from texts about the nervous system, and he had students read books about the nervous system on their own. Mr. Jeffers has a collection of books and allows students to choose from that collection for their independent reading.

Andrew chose *Another Day in the Frontal Lobe: A Brain Surgeon Exposes Life on the Inside* (Firlik, 2006) and regularly shares passages with his peers. For example, he read aloud the following lines to a classmate, Jessica, during free choice reading time in their English class: "We can thank, or blame, our frontal lobes for much of what we consider to be our personality and intelligence. Damage to the frontal lobes can be subtle, including changes in insight, mood, and higher-level judgment" (Firlik, 2006, p. 7).

In addition, Mr. Jeffers provided his students with vocabulary useful for discussing the central nervous system and, more specifically, the brain. He started with words used to describe locations: anterior, posterior, dorsal, ventral, rostral, caudal, coronal, saggital, and axial. He then moved to specialized and technical language including gyrus, sulcus, fissure, nerve, track, and ventricle.

Students kept journals and completed a number of writing tasks in preparation for the lab. For example, at the end of one of the class meetings, Mr. Jeffers asked students to identify questions they had about the central nervous system. He then collected these as an exit slip as students left class that day. He used these written responses to determine if students needed more information from him and to assess their developing inquiry into the nervous system.

In preparation for the lab, Mr. Jeffers showed his students a virtual lab of a sheep brain dissection (see www.academic.scranton.edu/department/ psych/sheep/framerow.html). For each slide, he shared his thinking. This think-aloud provided his students with an opportunity to understand how expert scientists think as they work. For example, when he displayed the first slide, he thought aloud about the physical orientation. As he said, "I can tell that this is the right hemisphere as I can see the rostral portion of the brain and I notice that the cerebellum is to the left. So, as I think about this image, I see that this part (points to top) is dorsal or toward the top. I see that this is ventral or toward the bottom. I also see that this is a saggital view, as if an arrow were shot from the back to the front and we were seeing that slice."

LEARNING IS BASED IN LANGUAGE

High-quality science instruction requires that students learn to read and write like a scientist. The discipline of science, and reading and writing in science, is different from history, English, mathematics, art, or nutrition. Science teachers guide their apprentices, students, in this discipline through reading and writing. That's not to say that science teachers should become reading teachers. In fact, we argue that not all teachers are teachers of reading (Fisher & Ivey, 2005). Instead, we understand that humans learn through language. As such, we have to ensure that students in our classrooms have opportunities to read, write, speak, listen, and view. This may sound like a semantic difference, but we think it's much more conceptual than that.

We understand that there are students who need access to reading instruction, even in high school. There are experts in reading who should provide that instruction, often in the English department. However, the job of the science teacher is a bit different. The science teacher has to provide students with opportunities to use language for learning content. Along the way, students will become better readers and writers. They will also develop a much deeper understanding of science when they are immersed in the language of science. They will begin to think, read, and write like scientists. Of course, most scientists in the "real world" read and write daily as part of their jobs. They write grants, reports, and articles. They take notes and organize information. They read the work of others and they read their own work. In fact, scientists read widely. We don't know a single bench scientist who reads from a single source. Scientists like to be informed, which requires that they read from a variety of sources in their discipline. Unfortunately, in many middle and high school classrooms, students only read from a single source and that source is most often the textbook. That's not to say that the textbook is bad. It's a great resource with tons of information and support. And, as we see in Chapter 5, there are ways to help students read from this type of text. We're just saying that it should not be the only text a student reads. Remember Andrew and his motivation to read widely such that he read from a popular press book about neurology? That's what we'd like all of our students to do.

Toward this goal of getting our science students to incorporate literacy as a scientist might, we acknowledge that educators must have an understanding of the various forms of literacy attainment. Shanahan and Shanahan (2008) have examined how literacy development progresses and conclude that there are three stages of growth that can be represented graphically in a pyramid form (see Figure 1.1). These stages are basic literacy, intermediate literacy, and disciplinary literacy. Basic literacy, the base of the pyramid of literacy development, represents the foundational and generalizable skills that are needed for all reading tasks—decoding skills, comprehension of print and literacy conventions, recognition of high-frequency words, and usual fluency routines. Additionally, students at this stage learn to recognize common ways to organize texts (e.g., story formats, list structures). These are basic literacy skills.

Figure 1.1   The Increasing Specialization of Literacy Development

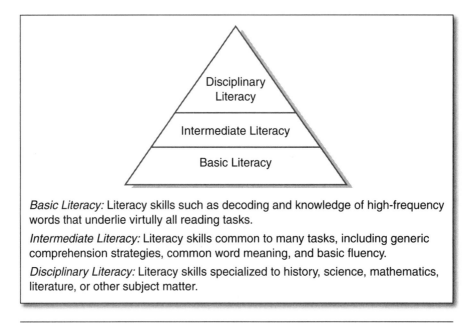

Basic Literacy: Literacy skills such as decoding and knowledge of high-frequency words that underlie virtully all reading tasks.

Intermediate Literacy: Literacy skills common to many tasks, including generic comprehension strategies, common word meaning, and basic fluency.

Disciplinary Literacy: Literacy skills specialized to history, science, mathematics, literature, or other subject matter.

Figure 1.1 from Timothy Shanahan and Cynthia Shanahan, "Teaching Disciplinary Literacy to Adolescents Rethinking Content-Area Literacy," *Harvard Educational Review,* Volume 78:1 (Spring 2008), p. 44. Copyright © by the President and Fellows of Harvard College. All rights reserved. For more information, please visit www.harvardeducationalreview.org.

As students progress beyond this stage—usually in upper primary grades—they move into intermediate literacy. This stage involves the development of skills that allow readers to facilely decode multisyllabic words, automatically respond to terms that are not classified as high frequency, understand the use of punctuation that is less common, and have a working knowledge of a larger body of vocabulary. At this point, students are better able to employ various comprehension strategies and can utilize "fix-up" procedures to mediate weaknesses in comprehension. Additionally, they are able to interpret more complex forms of text structure (e.g., cause and effect, problem-solution, parallel plots).

Beyond this stage, we move into an area in which content teachers are required to play a bigger role. This is the stage of literacy that we are most concerned with for science students at the secondary level. Shanahan and Shanahan (2008) call it disciplinary literacy. The skills involved in this stage are usually not formally taught and are difficult to learn due to the abstract nature of many discipline-specific texts. Moreover, disciplinary literacy is more constrained in terms of its applicability to a wide range of reading materials. Specifically, an English teacher who is proficient in teaching literacy skills related to reading classic and contemporary novels may not be so skilled at guiding students to comprehend a technical biology article from a current journal.

Consider disciplinary literacy in science. Content in science often requires reading between the lines, visualization, the interpretation of graphs and charts, and knowledge of inquiry methods of study. It is a process that differs greatly from that of reading *The Great Gatsby* or reviewing a primary source document like a speech written by Frederick Douglass. The progressive narrowing of Shanahan and Shanahan's pyramid represents the constricted and specialized nature of more advanced literacy skills—skills that are increasingly less generalizable to other areas of reading and more focused on the needs and skills of a particular discipline, like science.

USING LANGUAGE IN SCIENCE

By now you're probably asking yourself this: "How can I go beyond my current effort as I work to integrate language and disciplinary literacy into the science classroom?" This is what the rest of this book is about. Based on our experiences with hundreds and hundreds of students, we have some ideas about what works. To make our point, we'd like to invite you to read a brief excerpt from the U.S. Department of Labor, Occupational Safety & Health Administration technical manual related to Oil Well Derrick Stability.

> Supplemental footing shall be provided to distribute the concentrated loads from the mast and rig support points. The manufacturer's load distribution diagram will indicate these locations. In the absence of a manufacturer's diagram, the supplemental footing shall be designed to carry the maximum anticipated hook load, the gross weight of the mast, the mast mount, the traveling equipment, and the vertical component of guywire tension under operational loading conditions. These footings must also support the mast and mast weight during mast erection. (www.osha.gov/dts/osta/otm/otm_iv/otm_iv_1.html)

Conventional wisdom in many reading circles would suggest that the reader should deploy comprehension strategies to understand this passage. But we ask you, would making a prediction help you understand what the author wanted you to know? If not, how about summarizing or questioning or inferring or making personal connections?

This is our point in writing this book. Students often need more than simple comprehension strategies to learn. What would have helped you? More background knowledge is what you needed. As a result, our first content chapter, the one that follows this one, focuses on background knowledge. When you know something about oil wells, this passage becomes infinitely more readable.

Second, you might have had some difficulty with the vocabulary in this passage. You could probably read all of the words, but their specific usage might have confused you. For example, you probably know the word *mast* and you may have made a connection with a sailboat. However, the authors of this piece of text were using that word to mean a very specific part of the oil well. Thinking about sailboats wouldn't really help you make sense of the passage. In other words, you need vocabulary instruction, and not just a list of words to memorize, but rather meaningful interactions with words as they are used in the discipline. Importantly, we think of vocabulary as the expression of background and prior knowledge. Vocabulary is critical if students are to develop their understanding of science. In fact, it has been estimated that students are required to learn on average 3,000 new words each year in science. As a comparison, a Spanish I class introduces students to about 1,500 words. Science is a vocabulary dense subject area and we have devoted an entire chapter to this topic.

Once the reader has developed or activated background knowledge and has a sense of the words used in the discipline, reading and writing become much easier and more meaningful. Once background knowledge and vocabulary understanding have been developed, teachers can focus on reading and writing. We have chapters on both reading and writing in science that provide you with examples of instructional routines useful for students in learning content.

We conclude this book with a discussion of assessments. As teachers, we have to regularly assess student learning to make decisions about next steps instruction. The final chapter provides you with a number of ideas about formative assessments and using language to determine what students know and what they still need to know. As such, these assessment tools are part of the language system we use to improve student learning.

As we have noted, scientists read and write regularly. They have extensive background knowledge in their specific discipline and deep knowledge of the words used in their content areas. As science teachers, we can use these same processes with our students, apprentices in science, so that they learn at higher levels. Having said that, we're not suggesting that science become a reading and writing class. Students in science need to experience, ask questions, and interact. We're just suggesting that they do so armed with information useful in helping them inquire.

Developing and Activating Background Knowledge   2

Imagine that you are sitting in a beginning science class. You're behind a wooden table with your body crammed into a small plastic chair. Your instructor proceeds to discuss the topic of extraterrestrial geochemistry—a topic that is as foreign to most students as is the Latin language. He drones on about *lunar breccias* as if they were items you might find on any grocery store shelf. Next comes a vocabulary-laden presentation on the *tektites* of Western Australia. At no time does the instructor offer information that could bridge the gap between a student's lack of knowledge and the content of the day's lesson.

During such a scene, if you were to scan the classroom, you most likely would see your classmates engaging in one of the following: gazing off into space, doodling all over a note page, or sitting with knitted brows and a confused expression. Would such a situation be uncomfortable for you? Perhaps one or two people who happen to know a thing or two about geology or astronomy might be able to follow the lead of the teacher; most, however, would probably fall into a void of hopeless apathy or worse yet, a pit of frustration. Such a scene is the antithesis of what any conscientious and reflective teacher yearns for his or her classroom. Given the intense desire to avoid such a deadly scene, teachers must incorporate strategies that scaffold learning and provide background knowledge for students who find themselves tangled up in such a classroom quandary.

How can a teacher avoid being party to this kind of information delivery? How can he or she guide students as they build knowledge in a supportive and relevant manner? How does a teacher know what knowledge

7

to scaffold? The answer to these questions lies with the efforts of the teacher. An informed and rehearsed classroom teacher has the knowledge, the skill, and the ability to guide students toward an understanding of new terms. He or she can help students fill in background knowledge by providing opportunities to gain foundational knowledge that will aid in content understanding. It may sound a bit tricky, but the benefits to providing such instruction are well-worth the efforts.

WHY BACKGROUND KNOWLEDGE IS IMPORTANT

Background knowledge provides students with a foundation on which new content information, creative ideas, and critical thought may be built. A strong foundation is key to sturdy, lasting, and usable knowledge acquisition. According to Marzano (2004), academic background knowledge—what a person already knows about content related to school subjects like math, science, and English—correlates directly with academic achievement. It is likely that some students will have extensive background knowledge in areas that might not be school related. While such knowledge may be valuable to certain situations, our focus is on existing knowledge connected to the science content being taught in secondary classrooms. In many instances, science background knowledge is scant. Given the critical need for such knowledge, a teacher might astutely decide to engage students in activities that will subtly and cleverly support the augmentation of background knowledge. Repeated exposure to a topic will help the student store new knowledge in permanent memory (Medina, 2008). It is therefore imperative that foundational concepts are visited and revisited, especially by those students who have no prior experience with them.

Marzano (2004) notes three student-level factors that affect achievement: home environment, background knowledge, and motivation. While home environment is clearly an important factor, it is one that is beyond the scope of this book and is unlikely to be impacted by a science teacher. There are, however, ways that we can impact students' background knowledge. We want to address the concepts of motivation and background knowledge as intertwining factors affecting student achievement. We have found that there exists a reciprocal relationship between motivation and background knowledge. The motivation to learn clearly can lead to increased background knowledge. Likewise, having increased background knowledge can spark the motivation to learn more.

Most traditional classroom learning is dependent on extrinsic motivation. That is, students are propelled toward an end through the hope of a reward, or they may be driven by the wish to avoid a punishment

(Csikszentmihalyi & Hermanson, 1995; Kohn, 1993, 2002). For example, a student may work diligently in a particular class so that her "A" grade will reinforce her high status on a college application. Another student may complete a project so that he avoids being grounded for the upcoming weekend. These motivators are externally applied and often undermine the desire to learn (Csikszentmihalyi & Hermanson, 1995; Kohn, 1993).

Conversely, intrinsic motivation drives an individual to participate in an activity because he or she feels it is worth doing for its own sake. Rewards are typically nonexistent in such cases. Learning accomplished via intrinsic motivation is spontaneous (Csikszentmihalyi & Hermanson, 1995) and may be the underpinning for lifelong pursuits of education. Students who are intrinsically motivated tend to have higher achievement scores (Csikszentmihalyi & Hermanson, 1995; Csikszentmihalyi & Nakamura, 1989). Because the promotion of these types of scores is at the heart of what teachers typically desire for their students, the encouragement of learning rooted in intrinsic motivation is of the utmost importance. Finding ways to connect with student interests will enhance the probability that students can construct and store knowledge permanently. One way that motivation is expressed is through a self-actualizing experience or what Csikszentmihalyi (1990) calls *flow*. Flow is a state of concentration that results from complete absorption in an activity. It produces feelings of satisfaction that have underpinnings in motivation and interest. To experience flow, a person must be involved in a task that has the following: (a) clear, set goals; (b) resources to carry out the task in a way that allows the person to become totally immersed in the task; (c) focused attention on completing the task; and (d) immediate, incremental feedback, which suggests that the person is successfully meeting the goals of the task.

Note factor b. It relates to having the resources to complete the task. While this may, on occasion, mean that the person has physical resources, like a piano or a paintbrush, it also means that he or she has the skills provided by background knowledge to complete the task. Experiencing flow, an expression of motivation and interest, is clearly related to the possession of background knowledge.

To accomplish the task of motivating students so that they can build background knowledge (and building background knowledge so that they can be motivated), a teacher must embark on a two-step process. First, existing background knowledge must be accessed in an interesting and thought-provoking manner. A disinterested student will probably not care to expend the energy it takes to show off background knowledge. It is likely that a variance in the breath and depth of background knowledge will exist in any given classroom. A teacher must provide an opportunity for students to demonstrate their level of current knowledge. By doing this, the instructor can diagnose the next steps for individual students. An opportunity then exists for differentiating instruction for individual students. Once gaps in existing knowledge have been identified, a learning experience expressly designed to aid students to fill in the holes must be offered.

DETERMINING RELEVANT BACKGROUND KNOWLEDGE

To be able to provide proper background knowledge for students about to embark on a particular concept of study, a teacher must know how to assess prior knowledge. Such assessments need to be accurate and engaging, so that students are willingly motivated to participate in sharing what they already know about a topic. The types of assessments best suited for science instruction are discussed in the final chapter of this book. Having said that, there are ways in which the science teacher can quickly determine students' background knowledge, which we explore in this chapter.

DEMONSTRATIONS: UNDERSTANDING WHILE SEEING

Science teachers have long been advocates of using demonstrations. Demonstrations, alongside questioning, can provide a teacher with entry-level information while duly supplying students with content links. Demonstrations are typically used to display a theory, concept, or phenomenon (Fisher & Frey, 2004). They may be prefaced with preview questions such as *What do you think will happen?* or *Why am I going to do this next step?* Responses to such questions help the teacher determine what students already know. To use questions to assess all students and not merely those that are comfortable or keen on raising their hand to offer an answer, the teacher must find a way to allow all students to respond to a content-related query.

Probing *how* and *why* questions impel students to forward their disciplinary literacy skills. According to Moje (2008), a norm of practice in the discipline of science is to repeatedly study a problem before making a claim. Observable forms of evidence, such as those gathered through demonstrations, are commonly employed when studying a problem.

There are a couple of ways this may be accomplished. First, the teacher may offer the questions as writing prompts. Students may be given a few minutes to respond to an in-depth *how* or *why* question in written form. The teacher may monitor the progress of the class in an informal manner by moving through the classroom to scan student responses. Later, more time could be taken to look for misconceptions or areas that need clarification.

A second way to assess background knowledge involves asking students to share ideas verbally with a partner. Each person in the partnership is asked to respond to the teacher-designated question. Again the teacher monitors student commentary during the sharing time. If gaps in background knowledge are noted or if misconceptions are identified, the teacher may address such problem areas immediately. The monitoring process is the basis for the success of this approach. The teacher needs to be made aware of what the students think prior to beginning the lesson.

Here's how it works. Imagine that you are about to teach a lesson about Newton's Third Law of Motion. While standing on a skateboard, you push against the wall and ask students, "Why am I moving?" Students are then given a chance to respond in writing or as a sharing activity to the question. Up to this point, the scene is familiar. The teacher does a demonstration while students watch and try to figure out what's happening.

This is the turning point. The teacher usually allows one student to share an answer. Oftentimes this student is confident that he or she knows the answer. That's why the student volunteers enthusiastically. Sometimes the teacher will call on a student who may or may not be able to answer the question. The other students are left waiting. Some may be trying to figure out the problem; others may be tuning out. To really assess and then affect background knowledge, the teacher must ensure that all students are participating. Writing prompts and verbal partner sharing activities are key to involving all students.

In addition to this, the teacher must keep his or her eyes and ears open as students are monitored. Probing further with questions for individuals who need more direction may be offered when monitoring. Once all students have had a chance to think about and respond to the demonstration questions, the teacher may call on a student to provide an answer. If no students have the answer, then more scaffolding is needed. Returning to the classroom scene described earlier, if students respond in any of the following manners, the teacher has acquired key information that should direct or redirect instruction:

Q: Why am I moving? (when I stand on a skateboard and push against the wall)

Interpreting Student Responses

Response	*What It Means*	*What the Teacher Might Do*
You're rolling on the wheels.	The student understands that a smooth contact between two objects allows them to move past each other easily.	Provide other opportunities for the students to explain Newton's Third Law of Motion. For instance, a racket hitting a tennis ball or a hammer pounding a nail may be demonstrated as examples of the law.
When you push on the wall, you push on the skateboard and on your body. This makes you move.	The student understands that the push on the wall is making the teacher move but does not realize that there is a reaction force exerted by the wall on the teacher.	To emphasize the existence of a reaction force, ask students to pound their fist on the table (not too hard, of course). Then ask why they feel something against their hand.
When you push on the wall, the wall pushes back on you. You roll backwards because you are on smooth wheels.	The student understands that there is a reaction force and that the reduced friction between the wheels and the floor allows you to move.	Begin to introduce vocabulary that the students can use to describe what they are observing (Newton's Third Law of Motion, action/reaction forces, friction).

ANTICIPATION GUIDES: LOOKING FOR MISCONCEPTIONS

In addition to demonstrations and preview questioning, a teacher may use an anticipation guide to assess prior knowledge and uncover misconceptions. This is a teacher-prepared guide that is typically used to help motivate students and to provide them with a glimpse at upcoming content. In addition to these useful aspects of instruction, an anticipation guide is an excellent tool for determining background knowledge.

Anticipation guides require students to draw on background knowledge to determine whether a statement is true or false. In some cases, the student will need to make an informed prediction that will later be confirmed or refuted through new learnings in the classroom. This mode of thinking is characteristic of how scientists approach problems—by drawing on background knowledge to make informed predictions—and is an example of disciplinary literacy.

To develop such a guide, a teacher identifies major themes or ideas for the forthcoming unit of student/lesson. He or she then composes five to ten statements that can be used for a true/false or agree/disagree assessment. Some of

Figure 2.1   An Anticipation Guide for a Biology Class

Read each statement and decide if it is true or false.

True or False Before Reading		True or False After Reading
	1. Angiosperms include dogs, cats, ferns, and oaks.	
	2. Seeds form inside the flowers of plants.	
	3. A tomato is a vegetable.	
	4. The life cycle of an annual is less than one year.	
	5. Perennials remain alive underground throughout the winter months.	

the statements should be factual and others should be false. Prior to instruction, the students record whether they agree or disagree with statements. Using such an assessment, a teacher can target weak areas of background knowledge and modify instruction accordingly. Figure 2.1 contains an example of an anticipation guide used in a science class that is about to embark on a study of flowering plants.

A quick review of a class set of anticipation guides can inform a teacher of general class needs and also help pinpoint individual areas of weakness in terms of background knowledge. At this point, the teacher now knows what to include in the lesson plan. Following specific, prescribed instruction that has been developed in response to formative assessment, students may redo the anticipation guide to see their growth. It is expected that, after such instruction, students will know what they previously did not know about the topic. Knowledge of personal growth is a great factor in developing a motivation to learn.

KWL: USING KNOWLEDGE TO GENERATE QUESTIONS

A K-W-L chart, whose acronym lettering stands for *what do I know/what do I want to know/what have I learned,* is an informative tool for assessing background knowledge (Ogle, 1986). The first two columns of this chart are filled in by the student before the lesson. Students record all they know

———————— ✄ ————————

A K-W-L chart can be used to foster growth in basic, intermediate, and disciplinary literacy, depending on the focus of the content. If instruction is centered on simple definitions and foundational content, a student would be working at the lower levels. If, on the other hand, the emphasis is on complex content and inquiry-based thinking, the student could be moved toward intermediate literacy and even into disciplinary literacy.

about a topic in the first column and all they'd like to know in the second column. The information in the first column provides the teacher with clues to a student's background knowledge. If such a tool is to be used to assess prior knowledge, it's clear that the topic, which is provided by the teacher, must be obviously and accurately stated. It is critical that the teacher select key words that will connect with the curriculum. Such words act as a guide for students, letting them know what they should write about. Poorly chosen topics or key words will result in an inaccurate assessment of background knowledge. Figure 2.2 shows a K-W-L chart for the study of the periodic table in a chemistry class. To help isolate knowledge in specific categories, guiding points may be used as a suggestion to students to *think about* certain areas of importance.

Column 1 in Figure 2.2 shows that the student has very basic knowledge of the periodic table. She is superficially familiar with the structure, but she does not indicate knowledge of the specific organization of the groups or periods of the periodic table. Likewise there is no suggestion that the student is acquainted with the concepts of mass number or atomic number.

Figure 2.2 K-W-L Chart for the Periodic Table in a Chemistry Class

What Do I Know (think about the use, organization, and structure of the periodic table and be specific)?	What Do I Want to Know?	What Have I Learned?
• Used to organize elements • Has columns and rows • Has blocks for each element with information about the element	• Why is the periodic table important? • What do all the numbers mean? • Why do some of the chemical symbols seem so different than the names of the elements they represent?	

If all other students had similar responses to the question in Column 1, the teacher would need to begin with foundational information regarding the periodic table. If only a few students had gaps in knowledge, but many were familiar with much of the information on the periodic table, it would be logical to build on the existing knowledge by covering more in-depth concepts. Those few students in need of background knowledge would benefit from differentiated instruction provided by their informed teacher.

The second column of the K-W-L chart, *What Do I Want to Know*, is intended to impel students to think about the topic and to develop a motivation to learn. This part may be completed prior to the lesson, at the same time that the student fills in the first column. The last column, *What Have I Learned*, is, as with the anticipation guide, intended to foster a sense of growth in terms of content knowledge. This column is completed after the lesson and can be used as a formative assessment tool to plan additional instruction or determine which students need supplemental intervention.

WRITING TO LEARN: THINKING EXPRESSED THROUGH THE FINGERS

If further clarification is needed regarding a student's background, a Writing to Learn prompt could be introduced. Writing to Learn is an instructional routine in which students are provided with a prompt and directed to respond quickly, without undue attention to spelling and grammar, in written form. Well-chosen questions can be used with this format to further probe a student's understanding of a concept. Such questions would ask students to extend beyond the basic knowledge level of thinking. In science, well-crafted questions ask students to think about the mechanisms that cause phenomena to occur. A biology teacher might ask how viruses infect a cell. An Earth science teacher might ask why tectonic plates move. These questions prompt students to go beyond simple answers and require a response that makes connections between concepts.

For example, during an investigation about earthquakes, a science teacher wanted to know how much background knowledge her students already had. Given that they live in California, she assumed that they would know a lot. However, she didn't want to jeopardize her instruction by making a decision without data. As a result, she invited students to respond to the following prompt: What's happening below the surface when the earth shakes?

Armando's response can be seen in Figure 2.3. He clearly has some knowledge about earthquakes, but not enough for his teacher to gloss over this information. Armando doesn't really understand tectonic plates,

Figure 2.3   Armando's Written Response

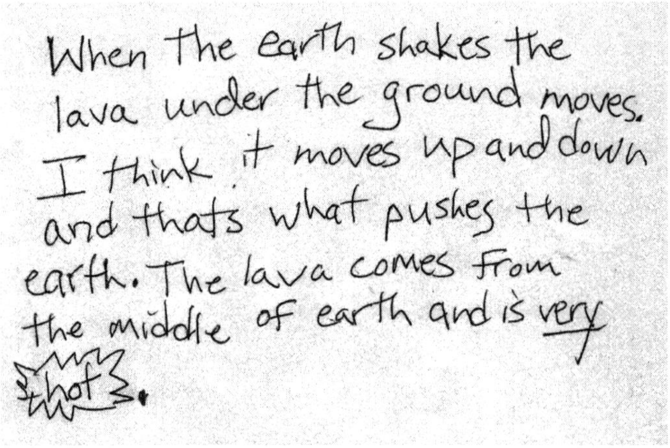

When the earth shakes the lava under the ground moves. I think it moves up and down and thats what pushes the earth. The lava comes from the middle of earth and is very hot.

their movement, and the resulting action on the surface of the earth. Additional information about writing in science is presented in Chapter 5.

ACTIVATING AND ASSESSING BACKGROUND KNOWLEDGE IN SCIENCE

The strategies discussed in this chapter—demonstrations paired with preview questions, anticipation guides, K-W-L charts, and Writing to Learn—are all particularly well-suited to science instruction. They all come under the umbrella of *content literacy instructional routines,* yet they are useful in developing students' understanding of science content. In the study of science, reading and writing are essential elements through which scientific principals are expressed, debated, and refined. Literacy and science are foundationally connected (Norris & Phillips, 2003). It's logical, therefore, that to get at what students know before instruction, a teacher must utilize common tools of expressing scientific thought— namely literacy tools. The structure of demonstrations with questioning, anticipation guides, and K-W-L charts provide students with ways to facilely record and organize knowledge and thoughts so that a teacher may review them easily. Because questioning is at the heart of science, it is especially apropos that questioning is at the center of the formative assessment being offered to students.

BRIDGING THE GAP WHEN
BACKGROUND KNOWLEDGE IS SCANT

Assuming that the teacher has successfully determined, through formative assessment, where gaps in background knowledge exist, how does he or she go about narrowing, or better yet closing, the gap? Many of the gaps could be narrowed at the very moment they are identified. If it becomes evident during a demonstration that students are missing a few small pieces of knowledge, the demonstration itself could be used to build new knowledge. Questions could be used to scaffold new information so that students, themselves, are constructing the knowledge.

For example, Armando's teacher might ask him to connect the movement of the molten rock of the mantle with the circulation of air in this way: "When I place a thermometer near the ceiling of our classroom, the temperature reads 23.5°C, and when I place another thermometer on the floor, it reads 22.0°C. What does this suggest about the movement of air? Using what you know about how air moves, what might you predict about the movement of the warmer and cooler parts of the mantle?" Such a line of questioning would ask students to use observational data to connect to new concepts. If large gaps in foundational knowledge exist, more serious and well-planned steps must be taken.

REQUEST: TEACHING APPRENTICES TO QUESTION

One extremely effective way to build background knowledge is called ReQuest (Manzo, 1969). ReQuest is a questioning tactic intended to support students as they examine new, and perhaps difficult, information, usually in text form. It is best to introduce ReQuest through teacher modeling. To model ReQuest, it is advisable to use a shared reading approach with a think-aloud component. Here's how this works.

A text is selected—one that offers students content that will help close background knowledge gaps. Next, paragraphs are chunked together. The first "chunk" is read using a shared reading approach. When a shared reading is conducted, the teacher reads the text aloud while students follow along by viewing the text while listening. Oftentimes the teacher will pause to clarify or ponder the content aloud. All of the teacher's thoughts should be articulated so that students can best understand how a proficient reader thinks as he or she reads. A shared reading offers students the opportunity to hear and see new or challenging vocabulary, provides clarification for novel content, and scaffolds an understanding of the techniques needed to read expertly. More information on shared reading can be found in Chapter 4.

———————— ✂ ————————

Questioning text material is a key component of disciplinary literacy in science. As they read, proficient science readers continually question the text. Sometimes questions can be answered by reading the text and sometimes they go beyond the text. ReQuest asks students to focus on the former type of questioning. The shared reading strategy, which is examined again later in this book, provides readers with opportunities to raise questions that extend past the content of the text.

When introducing ReQuest, a shared reading allows students to focus on content without encountering the "hang-ups" of decoding new words and interpreting text structure. Students can zoom in on novel ideas and phrase meanings. As the modeling of ReQuest proceeds, the teacher acts as the "respondent." In this role, he or she responds to questions gleaned from the chunk of text that was encountered in the shared reading. At this point, the teacher/respondent does not view the text. The students, the "questioners," provide the questions to the teacher/respondent. The questions are based on the text. Students are encouraged to reread and reexamine the text as they formulate questions. In this capacity, the students are thinking about the text, they're clarifying ideas in their minds, and they're making personal connections—all ways of building background knowledge. The teacher should respond as accurately as possible to the student queries. If a correct answer is not given to a particular question, the teacher/respondent may ask for a hint. The students may then provide one. If the teacher/respondent still doesn't have the right answer, the students may show where in the text the answer may be found. Following this, the teacher and students switch roles. The teacher asks the questions and the students, with texts out of view, respond.

Students should be given the opportunity to practice until they are sufficiently familiar with the roles of questioner and respondent. Using the gradual release of responsibility model proposed by Pearson and Gallagher (1983), the teacher may relinquish the responsibility to students once they have seen it modeled and have sufficiently practiced each of the components in a guided and directed format. In the case of ReQuest, the teacher may ask students to work in pairs. Students read chunks of the text and then alternate playing the roles of questioner and respondent. Within these roles, they examine teacher-selected text and build understanding in areas where knowledge was thin or nonexistent.

A teacher-led introduction to ReQuest might proceed like this: The teacher reads a passage that describes the properties of visible light from the text. As she reads, she stops when key terms, like "reflect" or "refract," are encountered, and she identifies the meaning of each as stated in the reading. She also pauses to clarify ideas by articulating thoughts such as *"It looks like light approaches a mirror at the same angle as it bounces off."* She then closes the book and asks each student to compose a question based on the section of the text that was read aloud. At first, the teacher might have the students write down their questions. This will give all students time to think and record ideas. Later, when students talk with a partner, they might just verbally state the questions for each other. A student-written question based on a text about the properties of light might look like this: *"Describe the difference between the incident ray and the reflected ray."*

Correspondingly, the teacher might respond as follows: *"The incident ray represents the light that strikes the mirror and the reflected ray represents the light that bounces off."* Students then verify that the response is accurate. While ReQuest is an exceptionally effective approach for building background knowledge, it's not the only one.

DR-TA: PREDICTING AS A KEY TO SCIENTIFIC READING

The Directed Reading and Thinking Activity (Stauffer & Harrell, 1975), also known as DR-TA, is a scaffolding technique in which students are guided to make predictions regarding a content-related reading and then asked to check their predictions. In this way students in need of bolstered background knowledge will be provided with an opportunity to themselves construct needed meaning. To have this kind of edifying impact on a student's knowledge base, the content reading must be carefully chosen by the teacher. The reading must provide the essential information needed by a learner as he or she proceeds to encounter new and challenging concepts.

A DR-TA should include the following steps: (1) Offer questions that guide students to use the structure of the text to predict upcoming content; (2) read a section of the text aloud and then ask students to confirm or revise their responses to the predicting questions; and (3) guide students to use their predictions and confirmed or revised responses to predictions to engage in a discussion of the content. Note that the students themselves are building background knowledge and are therefore becoming aware of what they already know and what they are learning through their reading.

As Fitzgerald (1983) noted, metacognition, the ability to think about one's thinking, is critical to increased comprehension. This is what you offer to students when you integrate a DR-TA into your curriculum—the chance to understand their own thinking in terms of comprehension. It's a skill that will pervade all aspects of a student's learning.

In an Earth science classroom where students are studying plate tectonics, a DR-TA might proceed in this manner. The teacher offers an engaging reading about the "Ring of Fire," a circum-Pacific trail of active volcanoes. The article discusses the unusual location pattern of these volcanoes and then connects location to plate tectonic theory. When a teacher first introduces a DR-TA, he or she must again model implementation. The goal, of course, is that students incorporate specific behaviors into their habits. In this case, the teacher would predict what the article was going to be about prior to reading. Bold print, photographs with captions, and italicized words are clues to meaning. In the case of the "Ring of Fire" article, a map of the Pacific-rimming volcanoes might prompt the teacher to speculate as follows: *"I wonder if this article is going to be about why there are so many volcanoes around the edge of the Pacific Ocean."* The teacher would then proceed to read a chunk of the text aloud so the prediction could be confirmed or refuted and revised. For this example, the teacher would verify that the article was indeed providing information to clarify the unusual pattern of Pacific-rim volcanoes. Prior to reading the next chunk of text, the teacher would again make a prediction, this time with the previously read content in mind. He or she might say, *"I think the next section will explain how subduction occurs."* The cycle continues with predictions followed by confirmations or revised thinking. Once the reading is completed, a discussion would ensue.

After the instructional routine is sufficiently practiced, the students themselves may read and complete the DR-TA cycle. As with ReQuest, a DR-TA provides students with a structured means in which to access content that will plug up the holes in background knowledge. Remember, the judicious selection of reading material is the key to scaffolding and building background knowledge.

QAR: CONNECTING QUESTIONS WITH ANSWERS

Question-answer-relationship (QAR) is yet another way to offer students an assembly pattern as they build foundational knowledge (Raphael, 1982, 1984, 1986). With the use of this instructional routine, students learn to identify four types of questions:

1. Right there

2. Think and search

3. Author and you

4. On your own

"Right there" questions are those to which the answers are explicitly found in the text. As a matter of fact, the phrasing of the answer is usually very much like that of the question. Students are most familiar with this type of question. Still familiar, yet a bit more challenging, are the "think and search" questions. These questions require that students read several sentences, perhaps even paragraphs of text, before they can derive the answer. Still the answer is expressly found by reading the text. "Author and you" questions require that the students draw on background knowledge to respond. Students are typically required to interpret or infer from the context of the reading. They make connections to themselves as they formulate a response to an "author and you" question. Finally, "on your own" questions prompt students to consider personal experiences. The text is used mainly as a springboard for thought. The response to the question lies solely within the realm of the student's own thinking.

How can QAR be used to bolster weak background knowledge? How can students acquire needed information to tackle more in-depth concepts? The answers to these questions again are in the hands of the informed teacher. A teacher who selects text material based on identified gaps in background knowledge is empowering his or her students to take hold of and control their own learning through structured reading, questioning, and thinking. As a building tool, an instructor may use QAR in two ways. First, he or she could simply engage students in a shared reading, formulate various questions, and then ask students to identify the type of question: right there, think and search, author and you, or on you own.

In an attempt to respond to the task, students will need to reread the text. They also need to think about their reading. These very acts ensure that increased comprehension will occur. Once students are familiar with QAR, a teacher could engage them in the second way of incorporating QAR—specifically, the teacher could ask students, possibly in small groups or with partners, to themselves develop all four types of questions for a content-based reading.

Imagine that you, the teacher, have provided your students with a reading on gravitation. The chosen text is designed to target identified areas of thin prior knowledge for the majority of students. You first engage students in a shared reading in which you note headings, bold print, and key vocabulary words. After reading, you proceed to ask the following question: "What is gravity?" In response to your own question, you answer as follows: "Gravity is a force exerted by all objects." The next question is addressed to the students: "What type of question was that?" Students skim the text to see that the exact answer is explicitly found in the text. On their papers they write *right there*. This scenario is followed by a series of question-and-answer sessions in which students are directed to identify the type of question. Figure 2.4 contains an example for how questioning might proceed in a QAR fashion.

How does this build background knowledge? Students are prompted to read and reread a strategically selected text. They cannot identify the type of question unless they know what information is actually in the text.

Figure 2.4   QAR Questions for Gravitation Reading

Question	Answer	Text	Type of Question
What is gravity?	Gravity is a force exerted by all objects.	Gravity is a force exerted by all objects.	Right there
What two factors affect the force of gravity between two objects?	The two factors that affect the force of gravity between two objects are the masses of the objects and the distance between them.	There are two factors that affect the pull of gravity. First, if the mass(es) of one or both objects increase(s), the force of gravity will increase. Second, as distance between the objects increases, gravity decreases.	Think and search
If the mass of one object is doubled and the mass of another is tripled and if the distance between them remains the same, by how much will the gravitational pull between the objects increase?	The gravitational pull will be six times greater.	The Universal Law of Gravitation states the following: Gravitational force = $(G \times m_1 * m_2) / (d^2)$. This formula may be used to calculate how much pull two objects exert on each other.	Author and you
Given that Pluto has a smaller mass than Earth, what kind of game could you invent to play in the low gravitation environment of Pluto?	Answers will vary. A possible response might be as follows: I would invent a game in which players, propelled by jet-fueled packs, carry a ball across the rocky landscape of Pluto. They have to have jet-packs to control their movement in the low gravity environment.	No part of the text explicitly talks about a game on Pluto. The respondent must compose the answer on his or her own.	On your own

In a guided manner, they are also instructed to read between the lines, especially when "author and you" and "on my own" questions are used. Granted, some students, those who have significant deficits in prior knowledge, will not be able to answer an "on your own" question and probably not even an "author and me" question. The point in this case is not that they can or cannot answer the question; rather it is centered on the ability to review the text to determine what is actually offered by the author. Those students in class who have stronger background knowledge will be afforded the opportunity to delve deeper as they think about possible answers to more text-implicit questions. In this way, QAR offers teachers the ability to differentiate instruction to meet the needs of all students—a powerful tool for every student in the class.

THE BACKGROUND KNOWLEDGE BIG PICTURE

Any teacher will acknowledge that some students come to the classroom door with scant background knowledge. Instead of allowing such a situation to continue to swell and wreak havoc for individual students, a teacher can choose to rectify the circumstance. Entry level assessment, assessment that is done at the start of new instruction, is clearly the first step. Use demonstrations with companion questions, anticipation guides, K-W-L charts, and writing prompts to target areas of weakness. Perhaps only a small group of students with gaps in background knowledge will be identified. In such a case, a small group intervention might be most appropriate. If, however, a majority of students are in need of action, a teacher should choose appropriate readings intended to allow students access to the needed knowledge. If such tact is taken, a scaffolding approach may be selected. ReQuest, DR-TA, and QAR provide structure, guidance, and opportunities for reflection—all aspects needed to foster reading comprehension. The tie between background knowledge and vocabulary is examined in an upcoming chapter.

Integrating Vocabulary Instruction Into the Science Classroom

3

When Jack's teacher, Miss Branson, reported that the viscous siliceous magma crept toward the surface, erupted, and was accompanied by a plume of ash that streamed into the atmosphere, Jack found himself overwrought with the thought of deciphering a sentence overloaded with new terms. As a matter of fact, Jack subconsciously took the route of so many others that find themselves confronted with strange-sounding, unfamiliar words. Specifically, he shut down and started doodling volcano pictures on the desktop. Jack's not alone in this classroom. Next to him sits Susana, a student who arrived from Columbia one year ago. Not only is she trying to acquire foundational English skills, but now she's also attempting to add content-specific terms so that she can survive in her Earth science class. There's no doubt that Miss Branson needs to use vocabulary specifically related to her content area. The big issue lies in her ability to support her students to understand what the terms mean. Stahl and Nagy (2006) make it clear that in terms of content area, *vocabulary* refers to word meanings. With this in mind, how would Miss Branson want Jack to respond to the question, "What does *siliceous* mean?" Is a mere definition of *siliceous* sufficient?

THE IMPORTANCE OF VOCABULARY

According to Merriam-Webster's Online Dictionary, *siliceous* means *of, relating to, or containing silica or a silicate*. Does a student who can recite that definition understand *siliceous* magma within the context of an Earth science class? Consider this—a *siliceous* magma is molten material found in the earth that possesses high amounts of silicon dioxide or silica. When this magma cools, it will form rocks that are rich in the mineral quartz. Most of the crust is made up of such rocks. Clearly the term *siliceous* has an intricate meaning within the context of geology. To merely provide students with a definition deprives them of the connections to ideas that are necessary for a full understanding of the term as it relates to the context. Memorizing word definitions simply does not work (Stahl & Fairbanks, 1986). To really grasp word meanings, students must store terms in semantic networks. Semantic networks are developed when words are connected to previously learned ideas, facts, or concepts (Fisher & Frey, 2008b; Stahl & Nagy, 2006).

Most likely Miss Branson wants Jack to know more than the simple definition of *siliceous*. She would want all of her students to be able to use the term in the conversations they generate, to understand the term when encountered in a text, and to conceptualize what the term means within the context of various Earth science references. This requires more than just memorizing a definition. It necessitates strategies that target word meaning and language acquisition. If Miss Branson truly wants Jack to develop a working knowledge of *siliceous*, she'll have to integrate specific vocabulary activities into her curriculum. Fortunately, this can be easily and seamlessly accomplished.

Before Miss Branson decides how to approach vocabulary instruction in her class, it's critical that she assess what students know at the start of the lesson. Consider the different ways students can understand a vocabulary term like *force*. A student might be able to recognize the term in print. He or she might be familiar with the concept but unfamiliar with the actual term used to describe the concept. The student might even be completely unfamiliar with the word and the meaning. Beck, McKeown, and Kucan (2002, p. 10) describe word knowledge along a five-point continuum:

- No knowledge
- General sense, such as knowing mendacious has a negative connotation
- Narrow, context-bound knowledge, such as knowing that a radiant bride is a beautifully smiling happy one, but unable to describe an individual in a different context as radiant
- Having knowledge of a word but not being able to recall it readily enough to use it in appropriate situations
- Rich, decontextualized knowledge of a word's meaning, its relationship to other words, and its extension to metaphorical uses, such as understanding what someone is doing when they are devouring a book

Within a science context, this might mean that some students would have no knowledge of the term *force*. Others might know that a *force* has something to do with science. Still some might know that a *force* causes a kite to lift up into the sky. Some might even understand that a *force* is a push or pull, but they may have difficulty recalling this when asked how a *force* might act on a soccer ball. The hope is that ultimately teachers will be able to guide students to a full and deep understanding of the term *force*. When this point on the continuum is reached, a student would know that a force exists in the form of gravity when a falling rock is pulled to the Earth. That same student would know that *force* could also mean *to bring about a necessary result* as in the sentence *John forced a smile at the end of his visit to the dentist.* The meaning of the term *force* is obviously dependent on the context. It's clear that memorizing a simple science definition is insufficient if the goal is to build word meaning.

VOCABULARY SELF-AWARENESS CHARTS

One of the best ways to determine what students know is to use a vocabulary self-awareness chart. This device is intended to guide students toward a realization of what they already know and an understanding of what they will be learning in terms of new words and their meanings. Figure 3.1 shows a vocabulary self-awareness chart for vocabulary words related to a unit that deals with the Law of Universal Gravitation.

A vocabulary self-awareness chart allows the teacher to determine what needs to be taught in a more systematic and intentional manner. Students

> A vocabulary self-awareness chart moves students into the realm of intermediate literacy by asking them to develop an awareness of both meaning and application with the content area. Students learn that words have depth in meaning. Additionally, they develop an understanding of the connection between context and word meaning.

Figure 3.1 Vocabulary Self-Awareness Chart

Vocabulary Term	Know Definition	Know an Example	Don't Know Either Yet	Definition	Example(s)
force		✓			pedaling my bicycle
mass	✓	✓		amount of matter in a substance or object	a glass of water, a balloon filled with air, and a rock all have mass
gravitation			✓		

completing a vocabulary self-awareness chart are more focused on the topic at hand. Additionally, they are guided to recognize that word knowledge extends beyond having a grasp of a mere definition. Students are led to understand that knowing the gist of a word is relevant and valuable, but there's more to truly knowing how, when, and why to use a word. Moreover, students learn that word knowledge is multifaceted and involves step-by-step action. It's far more complex than matching the word to the definition on the test.

CONTENT AREA WORD WALLS

To further advance this notion, teachers should consider posting foundational unit terms in a prominent place in the classroom as a word wall. The words can be viewed on a daily basis by the students and referenced by the teacher throughout the study of the topic. A word wall can act as a reminder that students should regularly see, hear, and use the words that are key to the unit (Harmon, Wood, Hedrick, Vintinner, & Willeford, 2009). A sample word wall from a physics classroom can be found in Figure 3.2. The teacher adds words to the wall on a daily basis and makes reference to the wall throughout the unit of instruction.

Figure 3.2   Sample Word Wall

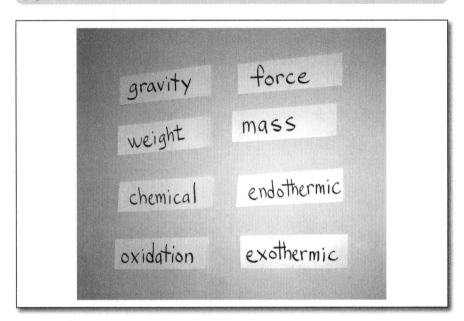

INSTRUCTIONAL ROUTINES USEFUL FOR DEVELOPING VOCABULARY

Once background knowledge has been activated or developed, the teacher may choose vocabulary activities that are best suited to accomplishing academic goals. Of course, this assumes that specific vocabulary terms have been identified. Fisher and Frey (2008b) identify a number of considerations for selecting vocabulary terms. The decision-making guidelines they developed can be found in Figure 3.3. In general, they suggest that teachers consider the following questions:

- Is the word representative?
- Is it repeatable?
- Is it transportable?
- Is it best understood by students through contextual analysis?
- Is it best understood by students through structural analysis?
- Does it overburden the cognitive load? (Fisher & Frey, 2008b, p. 27)

Mr. Cooper, an 11-year veteran of the chemistry classroom, knows that he must be selective when it comes to teaching vocabulary words. In chemistry, there are hundreds of technical terms that first year chemistry students need to acquire to ensure successful understanding of the content. In his attempt to maximize his vocabulary efforts, Mr. Cooper chooses words that represent the topic he is teaching. For instance, when teaching about the patterns of the periodic table, Mr. Cooper wisely chooses six to eight key words to highlight. The term *periodic*, for instance, is critical to an understanding of the organization of Mendeleev's table. An in-depth understanding of *periodic*, which means *at regular or predictable intervals*, can help students make connections to trends in atomic mass, electronegativity, and ionization energy as you go across or down the table. *Periodic* is clearly a term that will arise frequently when covering chemistry content. It can be transported to other areas in science. For instance, *periodic* could be used to describe earthquake activity in a region that historically has experienced seismic movements during fairly regular intervals of time. Additionally, the term can be transported and used in other content areas. It's a versatile term, whose meaning can be deciphered through context. Additionally, *periodic* can be analyzed structurally. *Period* is from the Latin *periodus*, which means recurring cycle, and the suffix,-*ic*, means pertaining to. Clearly, the term *periodic* would be a valuable one for Mr. Cooper's students to know as they pursue the study of chemistry.

SEMANTIC FEATURE ANALYSIS: ASSESSING RELATIONSHIPS BETWEEN WORDS

Once target words are selected, the teacher might use a Semantic Feature Analysis Chart (Pittelman, Heimlich, Berglund, & French, 1991). A Semantic Feature Analysis Chart has a vocabulary list in the left column and key features across the top of the chart. Students record a plus (+) if the idea or concept represented by the term has the feature and a minus (−) or zero (0) if the idea or concept does not have the feature. Students working with a

Figure 3.3   Considerations for Selecting Vocabulary Terms

Representative. This may be the aspect most frequently used by teachers when choosing a word for vocabulary instruction. Is the term representative of an important idea or concept? These words often come in the form of labels, such as *tectonic plate,* or *patriot,* or *parallelogram.* At other times, it may be a gateway word for a series of related words. For instance, teaching *create* can lead to a number of variants, including *creator, creative,* and *recreation.*

Repeatable. If the word is going to be used repeatedly, either within a unit of instruction or throughout the school year, it may be a good candidate for intentional instruction. Novel words that appear only once are not good choices because the learner won't receive multiple exposures to the word—a necessary condition of vocabulary learning (Stahl & Fairbanks, 1986).

Transportable. A third consideration in selecting a word for instruction involves transportability. Is it likely that this word will be useful in another learning arrangement, such as a classroom discussion or written assignment? Words that are transportable may be useful in other content areas as well, such as choosing to instruct on the word *temperate* in English to describe an even-mannered character, knowing that it will be useful in science as well.

Contextual analysis. This requires looking at the context in which the word is used, rather than viewing the word in isolation. If a term used in a reading is accompanied by surrounding words or phrases that define the word, then it is probably not necessary to provide direct instruction for this word.

Structural analysis. As with context, the structure of the word may be sufficient for your students to infer the meaning. This judgment requires that you know your students well, and are familiar with their exposure to the prefix, root, and suffix in the word. For example, a Civics teacher might decide not to explicitly teach *economic interdependence* because the affixes and roots present in this term are apparent.

Cognitive load. Unlike the other elements, consideration of cognitive load has less to do with the word itself and more to do with the learning context. At some point, the sheer number of words is daunting, and vocabulary instruction can detract from learning content—a bit like the tail wagging the dog. There aren't any hard and fast rules about what constitutes the "right" cognitive load, as it varies by learner and content. Our very informal rule of thumb has been to try to limit ourselves to 2–3 words per lesson, knowing that at some point students can't assimilate any more information.

SOURCE: Fisher, D., & Frey, N. (2008b). *Word wise and content rich: Five essential steps to teaching academic vocabulary.* Portsmouth, NH: Heinemann. Used with permission.

semantic feature analysis chart learn about the relationships between terms and the ways in which terms are unique. The repertoire of understanding broadens well beyond the recitation of a mere definition.

Consider this: Mr. Yee, an eighth-grade Physical Science teacher, wants his students to understand both the commonalities between various types of electromagnetic radiation and the differences. He decides to incorporate a Semantic Feature Analysis Chart for the first time in his third period class. To familiarize students withthe concept of a Semantic Feature Analysis Chart, Mr. Yee decides to show his students two examples with science content from sixth and seventh grade. His students are looking at a model of a Semantic Feature Analysis Chart that shows features of types of volcanoes (Figure 3.4) and one that shows features of cells (Figure 3.5). Mr. Yee then provides students with a structured version of the Electromagnetic Radiation Semantic Feature Analysis that has the terms in the first column and the features across the top. In a manner that scaffolds the procedures for completing the chart, Mr. Yee models how he uses the textbook to determine the features that are both true and false for radio waves. As he determines whether the features are characteristic of radio waves, he fills in a + or a – in each column (Figure 3.6).

When students write using a semantic feature analysis chart as a reference, they are typically synthesizing information about various related elements of a topic. The process of putting information together in a cohesive, logical manner is an intermediate disciplinary skill that, if conducted with a science-style writing format, could move into the realm of disciplinary literacy.

Figure 3.4 Semantic Feature Analysis: Volcanoes

	Key Features				
Types of Volcanoes	Formed by hardened magma	Gas-filled lava exploded into the air, cools, and falls back as cinders	Commonly occur within the craters or on the sides of other larger volcanoes	Erupts fast-moving, thin fluid lava	Tall, steep-sided volcano made up of layers of lava, ash, and cinders
Cinder cones	+	+	–	–	–
Shield volcanoes	+	–	–	+	–
Composite volcanoes	+	–	–	–	+
Lava domes	+	–	+	–	–

Figure 3.5 Semantic Feature Analysis: Cells

Type of Cell	Key Features						
	Has DNA	Has plasma membrane	Has cytoplasm	Has ribosomes	Has nucleus	Has organelles	Has endoplasmic reticulum and Golgi apparatus	Nucleus bounded by nuclear envelope
Prokaryotic cell	+	+	+	+	–	–	–	–
Eukaryotic cell	+	+	+	+	+	+	+	+

Figure 3.6   Semantic Feature Analysis: Electromagnetic Radiation

Forms of Electromagnetic Radiation	Key Features							
	Stream of photons	Related to heat	Can be used to cook food	Travels in a wave-like pattern	Seen as colors ranging from red to violet	Moves at the speed of 299,792,458 m/s in a vacuum	Can cause skin to burn	Can be used to view bones
Radio	+	–	–	+	–	+	–	–
Microwaves	+	–	+	+	–	+	–	–
Infrared	+	+	–	+	–	+	–	–
Visible radiation	+	–	–	+	+	+	–	–
Ultraviolet	+	–	–	+	–	+	+	–
X-rays	+	–	–	+	–	+	–	+
Gamma	+	–	–	+	–	+	–	–

Once Mr. Yee feels that students understand the concept, he allows them to work with a partner to complete the rest of the chart. Once the chart is completed, students are asked to use the information to respond to the following prompt: Describe the similarities and differences between the various types of electromagnetic radiation. Leanna, a 13-year-old sitting in the back row of Mr. Yee's class, consults her chart and begins to write about the similarities:

> There are 6 main types of electromagnetic radiation, including radio, microwaves, infrared, visible radiation, ultraviolet, X-rays, and gamma-rays. All are made up of a stream of photos that travel at a speed of 299,792,458 m/s in a vacuum. They travel as waves through space. Each type of electromagnetic radiation has certain characteristics. Infrared waves are felt as heat.

Leanna is clearly referencing her Semantic Feature Analysis Chart as she writes. It provides her with a structure for writing and with connections upon which she may elaborate.

Using a Semantic Feature Analysis Chart followed by an activity that utilizes the newly organized word information helps students, like Leanna, to present the meanings of key vocabulary terms in their own words. According to Graves (2006), students need to be involved in active, deep processing of such terms. There are many ways to do this, including having students follow up a vocabulary activity by responding to a short writing prompt. Another way involves having students put the definition of a word into their own words.

WORD CARDS: INVESTIGATING EXAMPLES AND NONEXAMPLES

A Frayer Model (Frayer, Frederick, & Klausmeier, 1969) is an organized format for guiding students to organize their understanding of a specific word using examples and nonexamples. There are several parts to a Frayer Model and teachers may tailor these parts to meet the needs of their individual students. Here are the basic steps:

1. Define the new term making certain to include key characteristics. For example, in a biology class students might need to know the term *mitosis* to be able to understand a unit that concerns genetics. A suitable definition would be as follows: *the process of division of somatic cells in which each daughter cell receives the same amount of DNA as the parent cell.*

2. Distinguish between the new concept and similar concepts. This, in many cases, can help to dispel misconceptions regarding word meaning. For *mitosis*, a student might write as follows: *this is different from the*

reproduction of germ cells, as you would find in the process of meiosis. Also, mitosis involves one cell division, not two, as in meiosis.

3. Give an example of the concept related by the term. For *mitosis,* an example might be as follows: *the reproduction of skin cells or heart cells.*

4. Give nonexamples of the concept related by the term. Again for *mitosis,* a nonexample might be as follows: *mitosis is **not** the production of sperm and egg cells because these require more than one cell division.* This process might take the form of first modeling nonexamples of a term, then presenting nonexamples alongside examples of the word while asking students to distinguish between the two. Finally, students would be asked to identify their own nonexamples. This step is challenging for many and requires modeling and practice.

To support students as they engage deeply with new vocabulary using the Frayer Model, it is often beneficial to have them make a visual representation of all aspects of the model. Figure 3.7 contains a sample Frayer card. The key term is located in the center of an index card and the surrounding four corners hold information related to the four aforementioned steps. Additionally, the back of the card can be used for a sketch that relates to the term. A series of cards related to a unit of study can be conveniently held together by a notebook ring or a brad. A collection of such cards can then be easily used for studying with a partner, for independent review of terminology, or for referencing when writing an essay or paragraph.

Figure 3.7 Word Card

Definition	Distinguish
The process of division of somatic cells in which each daughter cell receives the same amount of DNA as the parent cell	This is different from the reproduction of germ cells. Also, mitosis involves one cell division, not two.

Mitosis

Examples	Non-Examples
Skin cells	Sperm cells
Heart cells	Egg cells
Stomach cells	

SEMANTIC MAPPING: VISUALIZING WORD RELATIONSHIPS

Because it is critical for students to interact with new words on a variety of levels and within various contexts, Semantic Mapping (Heimlich & Pittelman, 1986), a method in which one word is targeted and connected to other relevant ideas and terms, can prove useful in supporting vocabulary acquisition. Stahl (1999) suggests that a teacher start out by guiding students to brainstorm or freely associate words connected to the focus term. A teacher may further facilitate an understanding of specific connections by suggesting relationships that are not offered by students during the brainstorm session.

In Mr. Gardner's ninth-grade Earth science class, students were asked to brainstorm words that connected with El Niño, a vocabulary term that had recently been presented to students within the construct of a large lecture class. Students had ample notes taken during lecture, from which they could garner ideas during the brainstorm. The brainstorm activity encouraged the review of notes, a fortunate by-product of this example of the Semantic Mapping process. Specifically, students had to refer to their lecture notes to come up with ideas associated with the phenomenon of El Niño. After scanning his notes, student Mario offered that, "an El Niño occurs as an oscillation, which means periodically or every now and then." "How often?" asked Mr. Gardner. "It looks like we have an El Niño every two to seven years," interjected Randy, a rather quiet, somber student who rarely contributed to class discussions. This time, the fact that Randy had notes from which he could refer, helped him conjure up the nerve to offer a clarifying idea. Tiffany added that "sea surface temperatures increase in the central Pacific Ocean." "Sometimes El Niño is called the southern oscillation," chimed in Christina.

Semantic Mapping clearly requires intermediate literacy skills. Students must establish connections between ideas by making decisions about what distinguishes one concept from another. This requires a student to compare, contrast, distinguish, support ideas, and provide examples so that they can graphically show relationships.

In less than 10 minutes, the students had generated a list that virtually explained every newly introduced aspect of the target vocabulary term, El Niño. In the end, Mr. Gardner saw only one hole in the patchwork of knowledge being woven together by the students. To help the students themselves fill in this gap, Mr. Gardner questioned them: "What is it that causes the build up of warm water in the central Pacific Ocean?" Several students lowered eyes to skim over their lecture notes.

Then Jack, in a somewhat unsure voice, queried, "Is it because the westward blowing trade winds slow down?" Before Mr. Gardner could confirm, Ingrid added, "Yes, that's what I have in my notes, too." After the brainstorm session concluded, students were ready to construct a semantic map.

The first few times this is done, as with any new instructional routine, it is best to model the technique and the thinking that supports the approach. After students become proficient in semantic mapping, a teacher might allow them to proceed with the development of a map with a partner or individually. The first time Mr. Gardner's students developed a semantic map, Mr. Gardner stood at the white board and *thought aloud* as he came up with categories for his map. *Thinking aloud* means that the teacher articulates what he or she is thinking about as he or she goes about an academic task, such as the development of a semantic map. The process of *thinking aloud* is explored in depth in Chapter 4, as it is a key to successful science reading instruction. Working in pairs, Mr. Gardner's students created the maps seen in Figures 3.8 and 3.9 using the relationships determined by the whole class.

Figure 3.8   Semantic Map Example #1

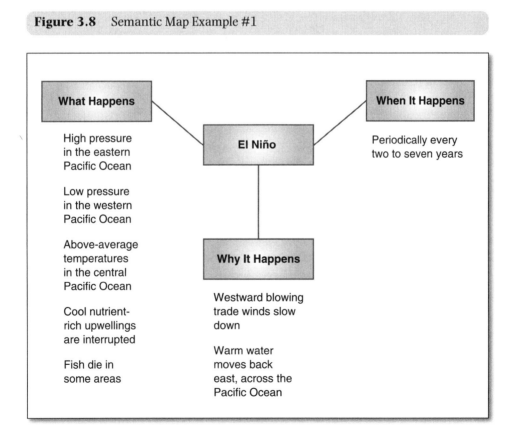

Figure 3.9 Semantic Map Example #2

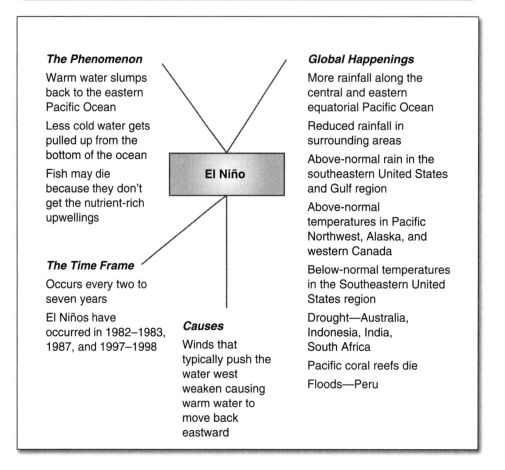

FOSTERING INDEPENDENT WORD LEARNING IN SCIENCE

Pick up almost any science text and you're likely to encounter, what seems to many, a barrage of daunting words like *decomposition, endothermic,* and *hydrolysis.* When Cherise encountered the term *polar covalent* when trying to read a chapter on chemical bonding in her oversized textbook, she felt the urge to slam the confounding book closed, toss her note-guide to floor, and for all practical purposes, conclude that she was unable to understand the book. Cherise threw in the towel. She gave up because she did not possess the deciphering skills needed to approach, decode, and acquire new terms on her own. While it's fairly easy to access any number of online dictionaries, when reading a science text it's really not practical to stop to look up every unfamiliar term. Such a task would make reading an extremely time-consuming and tedious event. On the contrary, to really understand and enjoy science, it's critical to have the ability to demystify the many new words that are encountered at a moment's notice.

Teaching students to break apart new words so that they can identify prefixes, root words, and suffixes is an essential aspect of independent word deciphering. When students know affixes (an all-inclusive term for bound morphemes, small semantic units that have meaning but never occur by themselves—e.g., *de* in *decomposed*), they are empowered to read and discuss science on their own. Additionally, they will no doubt have improved results on vocabulary and reading sections of several high-stakes texts, such as the SAT, ACT, and state achievement assessments—clearly a bonus benefit.

If Cherise's chemistry instructor had offered the class access to several key affixes and word parts, perhaps Cherise's response to the reading wouldn't have been so negative. Let's examine the offending term *polar covalent. Polar* means *having opposite ends*, like a pole. *Covalent* can be broken down to *co-* and *-valent. Co-* means *with or together.* If Cherise were reading about *polar covalent* bonding and she knew how to break down and decode the word parts, she probably would not have come up with the precise definition of the term, which identifies a bond between atoms in which one end is positive and one end is negative; she might, however, have been able to understand that the term represents a joining *together* of two atoms in which there are two *opposite ends.*

While this is far from a complete explanation of the word meaning, it is enough to satisfy a momentary need to understand a bit of word meaning as a term is encountered. Many times a reader, like Cherise, will understand enough to proceed with reading or with a discussion so that further, deeper understanding can be attained as more information is gathered. Basically, the ability to decipher words provides a student with the confidence and the basic comprehension to allow continued learning. The propensity to "shut down" is avoided and interest is heightened. When you know a little, you are more likely to want to investigate and find out more about a topic. Knowledge of word parts is clearly empowering and serves as a means of fostering increased independence. There are many resources available that provide lists of word parts, including the following online sources:

www.csun.edu/~vceed002/ref/reference/roots/chemistry_roots.pdf

www.etymonline.com/index.php

Cherise's teacher might have provided the class with a list that included the word parts like *hydro-* (water), *de-* (without), *en-* (in or into), *exo-* (out, outside, without), and *therm* (heat). Each unit in science will have a few key word parts that will aid students in vocabulary comprehension. Over time, a few words in every unit will add up to a large store of knowledge that can be applied to ongoing science reading and conversation.

In addition to teaching students to notice and decode word parts, it's important that they learn to evaluate the value of their word part knowledge

———————— ✁ ————————

By helping students to independently decipher science terms using affixes and various levels of context clues, a teacher is supporting the development of intermediate literacy skills.

in a particular situation. Most of the time, word part knowledge will prove beneficial. There are, however, occasions in which a reader's understanding of context will further help him or her to determine meaning. The prefix *hydro-* refers to water, and the terms *hydroelectric, hydrosphere,* and *hydroplane* all reflect the meaning of this prefix. There are, in some cases, terms that are anomalies when the prefix meaning is applied. *Hydrogenate,* for instance, refers to the addition of the element hydrogen. Despite the presence of the affix *hydro-, hydrogenate* does not directly refer to water. While there is a connection between hydrogen and water, it is unlikely that a student would be able to accurately predict the meaning of *hydrogenate* strictly by knowing that *hydro-* refers to water. More is needed in terms of strategizing and predicting. According to the research of Nagy and Anderson (1984), 25% of the time, word parts can be misleading. This means that, in most cases, deciphering terms using word part knowledge is useful. It is, however, beneficial for readers to have other tools at hand when encountering new science terminology.

One of the strategies that readers can hold in their stash of tools is the skill of using contextual clues. While seeking word meaning using the context of a sentence or paragraph can be useful, it's important for students to be aware of the fact the words surrounding a new term do not always reveal something about meaning. Specifically, science readers need to be aware of the four types of contexts identified by Beck, McKeown, and McCaslin (1983) that fall along a continuum of support. At the far end of the spectrum are the misdirective contexts—those that mislead the reader or suggest an incorrect meaning for a target term. An example of this would be as follows: *The lecturer paused for a moment and then **sardonically** said, "Galileo's critics were right on target."* One might think that *sardonically* has a positive connotation when in reality, it represents *disdain* or *mocking.* A reader would need to understand more about Galileo, his work, and his critics to detect the true meaning of *sardonically.*

Next along the continuum are the nondirective contexts. These contexts are of no help when trying to identify word meaning. An example of this type would be as follows: *The **velocious** movement of the car affected the travel time for the family. Velocious* could imply slowness, speediness, or even a zig-zag motion. The exact meaning, *speediness,* is not clear from the context.

Again moving along the continuum are the general contexts. These contexts provide clues that hint, with fair accuracy, at word meaning. An example of a general context would be as follows: *The player gave the soccer* ball a **hardy** *kick, causing it to fly across the field with great speed.* The reader would be able to determine that *hardy* meant strong or powerful because the ball moved with great speed.

At the final end of the spectrum are the directive contexts. These are highly likely to lead the reader to a real understanding of target term meaning. The following example shows a directive context for interpreting word meaning: *The increasing velocity and great mass of the truck caused it to have a much greater* **momentum** *than the slower, lower mass car.* In this sentence, *momentum* is directly tied to mass and velocity. In actuality, *momentum* is the product of mass and velocity. It's clear that while contextual clues are not always the best ways to determine vocabulary meaning, they can be quite useful in many situations.

Science texts in particular tend to offer clues that lean more toward the helpful end of the spectrum. Additionally, science texts will oftentimes have pedagogical contexts that are specifically provided to clarify meaning. For example, the following sentence is constructed to offer a definition to the astute reader: *The* **transparent** *lens, a lens that allows light to easily pass through, was used as an eyepiece in the telescope.* It's clear from this sentence that *transparent* means light can easily pass through a material. Teachers can guide students to understand that pedagogical contexts offer word meanings. Many times a key term is offset by a comma that is then followed by the word meaning.

WORD PLAY PROMOTES INCREASED VOCABULARY KNOWLEDGE

One way to help students build vocabulary and expand semantic networks is to have them create *word sorts,* an organizational structure in which vocabulary is separated into categories. This will support students in developing an increasing familiarity with the new words (Stahl & Nagy, 2006). Prior to her interactive lecture, Jackie Marshall asks her tenth-grade biology students to sort the following terms into categories: *mushrooms, yeasts, fish, amphibians, bacteria, blue-green algae, spirochetes, algae, funguses, protozoans, molds, mildews, mosses, ferns, woody and nonwoody flowering plants, sponges, worms, insects, reptiles, birds,* and *mammals.* Many students will simply separate the terms out into the categories of *plants* and *animals.* After a brief discussion of *kingdoms,* Ms. Marshall asks students to revisit their sorted words. They then have the opportunity to reorganize and relabel the words. This process allows students to tap into prior knowledge, to demonstrate that they've acquired new knowledge, and to make the connections necessary to develop a deeper understanding of new terms.

To further augment a student's ability to comprehend science vocabulary, it's important to spend time working with academic words. The Coxhead Academic Word List consists of 570 word families that were selected based on range of occurrence in 20 or more subject areas, frequency of occurrence, and uniformity of frequency in academic settings (Coxhead, 2000; see http://www.victoria.ac.nz/lals/staff/Averil-Cox head/awl/). Because there are so many identified academic terms, a science teacher should choose the words that are best suited for science writers. For instance, the academic words *hypothesis* and *identify* are commonly found in science writing. It would therefore be important for science students to make Frayer Models for such words, in addition to making them for the more commonly taught content-based terms.

Repeated exposures to target vocabulary words in context are more likely to result in real learning (Graves, 2006). The initial exposure familiarizes the reader. The successive encounters refine and solidify understanding. Many modern-day science texts provide an initial exposure that offers a pedagogical context so that readers can be introduced to the definition of a key term. This is often followed by an elaboration of meaning and is many times supplemented with a clarifying example. So what does this mean for those trying to teach science vocabulary? In essence, it means that students need to develop an awareness of the spectrum of context clues along with a metacognitive ability to identify the type of contextual clue offered by a sentence or paragraph. To best support students to develop this skill, a teacher needs to provide models of the various types of contextual clues that may be encountered. By simply taking a science text and reading aloud for students while noticing such clues, a teacher can support students in gradually attaining needed skills so that they can identify word meaning in an independent fashion. Once again, modeling followed by a gradual release of responsibility that moves the student toward independent practice of a cognitive strategy is by far the most successful way to help students attain a skill. The rate at which independence is achieved will vary depending on what is being taught, the age of the student, and the prior knowledge held. How to read aloud while modeling cognitive strategies, including the use of context clues to decipher word meaning, is explained in Chapter 4.

VOCABULARY HELPS STUDENTS UNDERSTAND SCIENCE

Vocabulary knowledge is foundational to reading comprehension for both English learners and native English speakers (Beck, Perfetti, & McKeown, 1982; Carlo et al., 2004). Because all branches of science are laden with subject-specific terms whose meanings hold the key to making connections between ideas and theories, teaching vocabulary is an underpinning of effective science instruction. Ultimately, the propagation of the nature of discovery and innovation will depend on our current students—those who will become our future researchers, authors, science professionals, and technology consumers. It is through an understanding of the language of science that our young people will be able to read, write, and engage in meaningful science-related conversations. Science issues, including topics related to energy supply and demand, water as a resource, genetic engineering, and air quality, affect us all today and will continue to do so well into the future. No one can afford to be without a basic understanding of science vocabulary. The more people know, the more they can participate actively in decision making for themselves and for society as a whole.

Reading Science Texts

One of the biggest obstacles to science instruction is the presence of the foreboding science textbook. Not only is it often heavy to carry around, but it also has the reputation of being difficult, boring, and hard to comprehend. How can teachers help the textbook overcome its bad rap? How can we get students to experience the fact that modern textbook production takes into account the diverse readership? In fact, many current texts incorporate strategies that support English learners, struggling readers, advanced students, and students with disabilities. The answers to these questions lie in the hands of teachers. If educators can employ effective instructional routines, in a manner that scaffolds the reading, to help students access text material in science class, then perhaps the reputation of the textbook and science content in general would be elevated to a status that claims the descriptors, *interesting, informative,* and *engaging.*

HELPING STUDENTS READ SCIENCE TEXTS

There are two questions to ask when approaching text that is particularly challenging. First, is background knowledge and vocabulary understanding adequate? Second, is the reading level significantly higher than the reading ability of the student? Let's examine the possible responses to these queries.

As we noted in Chapter 2, background knowledge of a content area is often foundational to reading comprehension, especially when a certain level of prior knowledge is assumed by the author(s) of the text. Many of us have found ourselves immersed in a topic of study for which we have weak or no background knowledge. Perhaps for you it was a calculus class or a world history course. If the background knowledge is scant, it is difficult, if not impossible, to approach a text that assumes you have previous experience with some of the content. Many texts at the secondary level, especially in science, are designed to take learning to the "next level." What if, however, a reader has holes in the patchwork of expected prior knowledge? What if the reader can't infer or read between the lines because the foundation on which to build the new knowledge is inadequate? Does this mean that the reader is doomed to forever being shut out of the content via the text? The answer to the latter question is *most certainly not!*

If it is possible for a reader with limited knowledge to learn more and new content, how then can an educator facilitate such an occurrence? In many instances, a reader is simply in need of alterative types of texts that provide high levels of content at lower reading levels. Attention to the gaps in critical knowledge need to be offered, so that bridges can be built to straddle blocks of content knowledge that need to be connected. It's really about building semantic connections to new knowledge. If there is no existing schema, the webs of knowledge won't hold together. Building the foundations on which a web of knowledge can be expanded is critical and doable when a concerned educator steps in with a reading intervention plan.

In science, in particular, finding high content information that is accessible at lower reading levels takes effort, but it is possible. The International Reading Association (IRA) regularly publishes *teachers' choices* book lists, many of which are science trade books (www.reading.org). There is also an award for nonfiction writing, the Orbis Pictus, which recognizes excellence in social studies and science writing (see www.ncte.org/awards/orbispictus). Once a teacher locates material that is at an appropriate reading level, how can he or she help students access the content? There are two research-based instructional routines that can do just this: (1) read-alouds and (2) shared readings. Each of these needs to be implemented with thought, preparation, and the proper mechanisms or scaffolds in place.

READ-ALOUDS SUPPORT STUDENT LEARNING

A read-aloud is an instructional routine in which the teacher reads a piece of text—narrative or informational—to students. Typically, students do not see the text while the reading is being conducted. They simply hear the teacher read and are able to focus on listening to fluid reading offered by a proficient, well-rehearsed reader. The emphasis is on presenting content and building critical thinking skills.

Mr. Wayne Davidson has taught chemistry to eleventh graders for seven years. Every school year he encounters students in his classroom who lack basic, yet critical, knowledge regarding atoms, electrons, protons, and neutrons—content that most students are introduced to in elementary school and then again in eighth grade. As a part of his curriculum, Mr. Davidson's end goal is to help students acquire a working, in-depth knowledge of the periodic table. With this in mind, Mr. Davidson knows that finding ways to help students build prior knowledge is of prime importance. To accomplish this, he has sought out trade books that will allow his students to build the foundation that is necessary to support the higher level of content understanding that is ultimately the goal. Mr. Davidson uses carefully selected trade books to help students bridge gaps in knowledge, acquire needed vocabulary, and foster critical thinking and inquiry skills. There are several specific strategies that Mr. Davidson employs to accomplish these goals via a read-aloud.

When Mr. Davidson teaches concepts related to the periodic table, he regularly chooses to read excerpts from the trade book by Salvatore Tocci (2004), *The Periodic Table*. Why does Mr. Davidson use this text to introduce the ideas related to groups, periods, metals, and nonmetals? He does this simply because the text is approachable, relevant, and introduces needed concepts in a relatable, cohesive manner. To contrast, Mr. Davidson's classroom textbook is densely packed with technical vocabulary and concepts that build on assumed prior knowledge. By broaching the topics that are foundational to an understanding of the periodic table in an engaging and accessible way, students like Jaleesa and Alberto can be prompted to construct basic knowledge onto which increasingly more complex concepts can be built.

> Read-alouds may be used to fill in gaps in basic literacy. Students who are not fluidly able to read science text on their own are afforded the opportunity to hear and reflect on the content. Discipline-specific vocabulary can be emphasized by the teacher as he or she reads, providing a means by which to move students up the pyramid into intermediate and disciplinary literacy domains.

When Mr. Davidson introduces the periodic table to his chemistry students, he begins by asking students to explain, in some fashion, how the homes and buildings in the neighborhood are arranged. As students flesh out their ideas on paper, Mr. Davidson walks around the room, observing both sketches and written descriptions. He allows students to respond in various ways—some through drawing and others through written word. When Mr. Davidson is satisfied that all students have their ideas down, he asks them to share their responses in groups of four. Because having small group conversations is a regular occurrence in Mr. Davidson's class, students immediately know where to turn and with whom to speak. As a result, the transition from independent work to group conversation is smooth and quick. Jaleessa tells her group that the neighborhood is made up of street blocks that form squares. She adds that there are about seven or eight buildings on each block. Alberto shows his sketch—a rough penciled—in drawing that clearly displays a diagram depicting exactly what Jaleesa has described.

Next, pointing to a chart on the wall, Mr. Davidson asks the class to think about how the periodic table is arranged. The students are then instructed to jot down their thoughts onto a piece of paper. At this point, Mr. Davidson brings in the trade book, *The Periodic Table* (Tocci, 2004). He begins to read:

> Do the students in your classroom have assigned seats? If they do, your teacher probably had some logical reason for assigning students to their seats. For example, your teacher may have arranged the seats based on the spelling of students' last names. Perhaps your teacher arranged the seats based on students' height, with the shorter ones sitting in the front of the classroom. (pp. 5–6)

Here Mr. Davidson pauses, directs students to view the oversized periodic table on the wall, and begins to point out the rows, called *periods,* and the columns, known as *groups.* He explains to his students that they will read about how the arrangement of the periodic table represents a logical organization system that categorizes elements according to the number of particles, called protons, found in their nuclei and according to specific characteristics related to the electrons in the outer shells of the elements. As he mentions new terms, like *period,* Mr. Davidson pulls out a word strip with the term legibly printed on cardstock with an adhesive magnet glued to the back. He slaps the word strip onto the white board and says, "This is a term you will soon know and be able to use in your chemistry conversations." With that, Mr. Davidson continues his read-aloud.

According to Ivey and Broaddus (2001), middle school students greatly enjoy having a teacher read aloud to them. Although reading aloud to students in a classroom might seem easy and effortless, a well-presented, meaningful read-aloud takes planning, practice, and a great deal of forethought. A synthesis of current research suggests that teachers should take the following steps when planning and implementing a read-aloud (Albright & Ariail, 2005; Fisher & Frey, 2004; Lapp & Flood, 2005):

1. Practice prereading the text. Focus on inflection, intonation, mood, word pronunciation, and decide where to pause to provide student reflection opportunities.

2. Establish the purpose for reading. Students need to explicitly see how a read-aloud text relates to the prescribed course content and the objectives of the course.

3. Model how to ask questions by thinking aloud as you read. Articulate not only the questions but also the answers. Reveal how you determine author intent, clarify meaning, and persevere in reading even when the text seems complex or challenging. Show how you draw on your own prior knowledge when reading.

———————— ✄ ————————

Step 3 of the read-aloud protocol provides an opportunity for a teacher to scaffold and support the acquisition of disciplinary literacy. For instance, a teacher could pause while reading to predict and then later confirm information. Predicting following by confirmation of information is a common action for science readers.

4. Allow time for students to make connections to the text. Be sure to model this, so that students can see how to tap into background experiences, how to link to previously learned content, and how to construct new knowledge.

5. Require students to re-present text information in another format (poster, verbal or written summaries, graphic organizers, etc.). This fosters critical thinking, encourages conversation founded in content, and ensures that students create a usable record of the read-aloud content.

While many teachers read aloud to their students, clearly not all are investing time in advanced preparations (Albright & Ariail, 2005). A weakly delivered read-aloud, one in which words are mispronounced, new vocabulary is not discussed, a monotone voice is used, or the flow is interrupted, will fizzle and fall flat. On the other hand, read-alouds done well provide opportunities for engagement, inquiry, new learnings, and increased connections to content. They are worth the investment of time.

When Mr. Davidson asked his students to think about the ideas of *arrangement* and *organization* in their environment, he was establishing the purpose for the read-aloud. Mr. Davidson wanted students to see that there is a connection between the familiar setup of organized neighborhoods and the structure of the periodic table. Mr. Davidson had practiced his read-aloud numerous

———————— ✄ ————————

When reading aloud to students, a teacher can model how to make connections to prior knowledge, an intermediate literacy skill that provides the foundation for further movement into the realm of disciplinary literacy. Science readers always layer new knowledge on top of and in between prior knowledge as they build and fill in semantic networks.

times. He knew where he wanted to pause for discussion, and he stopped at predetermined points to focus on key vocabulary. When Mr. Davidson came across concepts in the text that related to previously learned content, like the structure of atoms, he explicitly showed how he made connections to his prior knowledge. For example, at one point, Mr. Davidson recalled aloud, "I remember last year when we looked at the structure of an atom. The nucleus contains the protons and neutrons, while the electrons can be found in energy levels that surround the nucleus." Then Mr. Davidson queried himself by saying, "I wonder if the structure of an atom relates to where it is located on the periodic table." Following this comment, he continued to read.

After Mr. Davidson finished the selection, he wanted students to think about what they had just heard. To solidify the concepts that students should have become familiar with as a result of the reading, Mr. Davidson asked his students to record salient ideas in a graphic organizer format. They worked with partners on this and created collaborative records of what they had learned. Figure 4.1 contains an example from a student.

Now that Mr. Davidson had generated interest, fostered content-related conversations, and helped his students tap into existing prior knowledge and build new background knowledge, he was ready to introduce more in-depth, challenging content using the state-adopted textbook. To do this, Mr. Davidson used a shared reading and think-aloud model.

Figure 4.1   Example of a Student-Generated Record of Read-Aloud Information

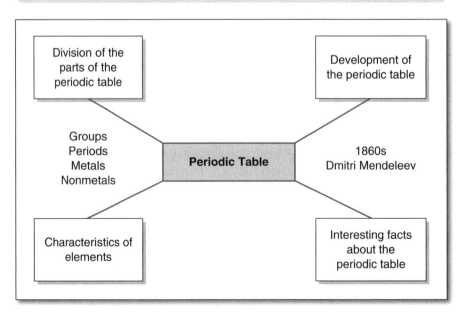

SHARED READING DEFINED AND IMPLEMENTED

When a teacher reads aloud to students and both simultaneously see the text, this is called a shared reading. Mr. Davidson begins his shared reading by telling his students that he is going to let them hear what is going on in his head as he reads a challenging text. By doing this he can model how to predict, think critically, utilize text features, and persevere even when encountering difficult words, phrases, and ideas. Here's what Mr. Davidson articulates as he begins his reading:

> Looking over these first few pages, I see that there is a heading in bold print, a figure with a caption, and an italicized vocabulary list. The heading is, "The Organization of the Periodic Table." I'm probably going to learn about the rows and the columns of the periodic table. Next I see a figure with a caption that reads, "Families of the Periodic Table." The figure is of the periodic table and there are headings pointing to several columns and rows. These headings include alkali metals, alkaline earths, noble gases, halogens, lanthanides, and various other terms. I'm also noticing that these are the same terms found in the vocabulary list. I wonder if I'm going to learn about the families and the characteristics they possess?

Mr. Davidson pauses here to share with his students a bit more about this metacognitive activity. He tells students that he is revealing what he typically does before he actually reads a science text. Specifically, he is previewing figures, headings, and new terms, and he is predicting what will be presented in the text.

At this point, Mr. Davidson continues his shared reading by delving into the actual reading:

> "*The periodic table is organized across rows by increasing atomic number.*" I remember when we talked about atomic numbers yesterday. The atomic number is equal to the number of protons in the nucleus. In a neutral atom, this equals the number of electrons in the atom. "*As you go across rows, the chemical and physical properties of the elements change and repeat. Each sequence of elements can be placed in a row called a period.*" So the rows are called periods. I guess the term *period* has more than one meaning. In my English studies, a *period* has always been an end-mark at the close of a sentence. In science, it represents a row on the periodic table.

———————— ✿ ————————

Science texts often have charts, graphs, and tables. A proficient science reader will read the text that correlates to a chart, for instance, and then study the chart, looking for key labels, units of measure, data values, and so forth. He or she then will go back to the text to reread or continue reading. This type of reading—science-style reading—can be modeled during a think-aloud shared reading. It will help students move toward disciplinary literacy proficiency.

Mr. Davidson continues in this manner. He reads and then pauses to clarify meaning. He connects to prior experiences and frequently stops to focus on new vocabulary. Mr. Davidson's intent is to show students that proficient readers think about the text as they read. They negotiate meaning and recall previous learnings. They also ask questions and predict upcoming content in the text. Further along in the reading, Mr. Davidson makes note of particular text structures—those that are characteristic of science writing.

For instance, when Mr. Davidson comes across this phrase in the text, "If there are seven electrons in the outer energy level of the atom, then the atom could bond with another atom that has one electron in its outer energy level," he explains that, in science, one event is often dependent on another. Such a situation is commonly signaled by the text structure *if-then*. Mr. Davidson refers to the sentence he has just read and summarizes the idea of the *if-then* sentence in his own words: "If an atom has seven electrons in its outer shell, it needs one more to have a full shell of eight electrons. Then it can join with an atom that has one electron available in its outer shell." Again, students were able observe how Mr. Davidson is thinking critically about the text and how he is negotiating meaning in a reflective and explicit manner.

THE BENEFITS OF SHARED READING

———————— ✿ ————————

A teacher who models how to use clues and cues provided in textbooks is helping his or her students understand how to tackle content-based information. There are common elements featured in science readings that an astute teacher might highlight. For instance, when reading a graph, a science reader would make mental note of the title, axes, units of measure, and changes of the line, bars, or pie slices. During a shared reading, the teacher-reader should pause to pay attention to these elements—elements that many inexperienced readers will skip over.

Shared reading is an effective instructional routine when a teacher wants to guide students to tackle difficult texts (Hicks & Wadlington, 1994). Not only are science textbooks loaded with new and usually unfamiliar terminology, but they often assume that the reader possesses a certain level of background knowledge. By modeling how a reader can approach such a text, how familiar root words can be used to decipher new vocabulary, and how good readers move forward in spite of the fact that they are occasionally confused by text and unsure of meaning, Mr. Davidson is helping his students see how independent readers read. Perseverance is clearly a key component of reading. Mr. Davidson knows that by continuing to read on, even in the face of temporary confusion, a reader can oftentimes find clarity and understanding in upcoming content or from a look at figures, diagrams, and captions. Textbooks provide numerous cues and clues for unraveling the meaning of content topics, like periodicity and chemical bonding. Mr. Davidson also knows that sometimes he has to refer to other books or online resources to clarify confusing concepts. To model this, Mr. Davidson picks up a dictionary and looks up the word *valence.* He reads the definition aloud and then persists in his reading. Looking up from the text for a moment, he says to the students, "Sometimes good readers need to look up new words."

RELEASING RESPONSIBILITY TO STUDENTS

Once students have had the opportunity to see what successful readers do to prepare for and engage in reading, they need time to practice. Fisher and Frey (2008a) developed an instructional protocol, based on the Gradual Release of Responsibility model (Pearson & Gallagher, 1983), which suggests that students need to experience learning in various ways before they can actually acquire a cognitive strategy that they can use in a seamless, natural manner. This instructional model consists of four components: *focus lessons, guided instruction, collaborative learning,* and *independent work.*

Focus lessons are intended to set the stage for the learning. Students are asked to tap into prior knowledge and focus on what they will be learning. Oftentimes this includes looking at the big ideas that will be studied in upcoming lessons. Mr. Davidson clearly had this in mind when he strategically chose a trade book that would help students build the background knowledge they needed to proceed with the content. Recall that Mr. Davidson pointedly asked his students to focus on arrangement and organization. This was in strategic preparation for lessons that would help students develop an understanding of the structure of the periodic table. Mr. Davidson realized that if students understand the organization of this chart, they will be better prepared to use it to predict the types of chemical bonds that might be formed and the resultant compounds that could be produced. Additionally, this type of lesson sets the stage for more work dealing with chemical reactions. It truly is foundational, and consequently, the presentation of overarching questions and ideas and the methods used to foster critical thinking are of prime importance.

When Mr. Davidson asked his students to listen in and participate as he revealed the questions, the connecting ideas, and the clarifying thoughts that crossed his mind as he read the periodic table chapter of the classroom textbook, he was providing an opportunity for students to engage in **guided instruction.** Students were able to see how Mr. Davidson managed to make meaning out of content-heavy text loaded with technical vocabulary. To transition students to a more independent position—one in which they could take the reins, question the reading, and make meaning themselves—he offered more and more opportunities for students to work with him as he conducted the shared reading. To facilitate this, Mr. Davidson paused several times during the reading and asked students to look at the next bold subtitle, predict what will be read in the upcoming text, and then share ideas with a partner.

For example, when he came across the term *chemical bonding,* Mr. Davidson asked students to clarify the meaning of the term using their background knowledge and an understanding of the common usage of *bonding.* All students were in agreement when their fellow student, Ruby, explained that *bonding* has occurred between herself and her lab partners: "We share something in common. We all want to work together to do well on our labs and to learn something new about chemistry. Maybe *chemical bonding* is a relationship or something shared between atoms that join together." Students were allotted time and given a structure for practicing predicting and clarifying meaning.

FACILITATING COLLABORATIVE LEARNING

Once Mr. Davidson and his students had finished the shared reading, it was time for them to wrestle with the content through a **collaborative learning** conversation with their peers. Mr. Davidson has a variety of discussion structures that he uses to facilitate conversations, including ReQuest (Manzo, 1969) and Reciprocal Teaching (Palincsar & Brown, 1984).

REQUEST: READING WITH QUESTIONS

In addition to using ReQuest to activate and build background knowledge, this instructional routine can be used to develop cognitive reading strategies as students practice asking and answering questions. When doing ReQuest, Mr. Davidson will have students work with a partner to read a text. One person will act as the *questioner,* while the other is the *respondent.* To support all students in his class, Mr. Davidson will sometimes differentiate his lesson by choosing readings that best meet the needs of his students.

For instance, if Mr. Davidson has a couple of students who are struggling with understanding the basic ideas behind atomic structure, he will pair these students and provide them with a text that is at their reading level and that provides content to help bridge the gap in prior knowledge. At the same time, Mr. Davidson might have students in his class who are advanced in their knowledge regarding the periodic table and valence numbers. For such students, Mr. Davidson would provide readings that take them into chemical bonding in great detail.

To use ReQuest, Mr. Davidson often provides cue cards laminated on card stock for each student (Figure 4.2). The *questioner* receives cards that direct him or her to read a chunk of the text, think about two or three questions to ask his or her partner, and then check to be sure that the partner knows the right answer. The *respondent* receives a card

Oftentimes, questioning strategies like ReQuest and reciprocal teaching are used to encourage students to ask questions that can be answered by reading the text. To move these strategies toward the disciplinary literacy sphere, a teacher should encourage students to do as scientists do—ask questions that go beyond the text. Even better, ask questions that might require further research to be answered. Scientists typically read background material and previously conducted research as a means to developing researchable questions that further the field of study. Perhaps students could even conduct research based on questions they develop while reading.

that directs him or her to read the same chunk of text, think about two or three questions that he or she might be asked, and then respond when asked the questions by the partner. There is no place for failure in this activity. If the *respondent* can't answer the question, the *questioner* is allowed to provide a hint or to show his or her partner where the answer can be found in the text. The ultimate goal is to get students to read a text, think about its content, and discuss it with a partner. As a part of this, teachers will see that students read, reread, and record notes as they are reading—all tasks that advance student thinking.

Figure 4.2   Cue Cards for ReQuest

Questioner	Respondent
1. Read a chunk of text silently and think of two or three questions to ask your partner.	1. Read a chunk of text silently and think of two or three questions that your partner might ask you.
2. With the text in front of you, ask your partner to answer each of your questions.	2. Cover the text and try to answer each of your partner's questions.
3. If you partner needs a *hint*, you may provide one.	3. If you need a *hint*, you may ask your partner for one.
4. If your partner needs more help, you may show him or her where the answer may be found in the text.	4. If you need more help, you may ask your partner to show you where the answer may be found in the text.

ReQuest is a straightforward, effective structure to facilitate student conversations. In science, ReQuest can be used to help students negotiate content meaning, decipher vocabulary, and review previously learned information. The intent is determined by the teacher, who purposefully selects readings that will help students accomplish any or all of the afore-mentioned goals.

RECIPROCAL TEACHING: PRACTICING WHAT GOOD READERS DO

Sometimes Mr. Davidson asks his students to work in groups of four to read and discuss a text. To do this, he often employs an instructional routine called Reciprocal Teaching. To implement Reciprocal Teaching, Mr. Davidson again selects an appropriate text—one that meshes with his course goals. Next he organizes students into groups of four. Typically his groups consist of heterogeneous mixes of students on all levels (English proficiency, content knowledge, and reading ability). Reciprocal Teaching directs students to think about several aspects of reading, including the following:

1. Predicting: Using cues from both words and features (e.g., bold print, headings, and figures), students anticipate and forecast what will happen next.

2. Clarifying: When students encounter a word or phrase that is confusing or unclear, they use context clues, knowledge of root words and word parts, and help from others in the group to decipher meaning. In some cases, they simply acknowledge the need for further clarification and must persist with the reading until future opportunities to clarify are presented.

3. Questioning: Students read a chunk of text, then create a question or two that correlates with the reading. They answer their own questions as they read, or they may develop questions that could be answered through further reading or research.

4. Summarizing: Students summarize content as they read by noting key ideas and themes.

At first, Mr. Davidson asks his students to do one of the following tasks for a series of chunked pieces of text: *predict, clarify, question,* or *summarize.* Each time a student group does Reciprocal Teaching, the individuals in the group change roles so that every student gets the opportunity to practice all tasks. Eventually Mr. Davidson tells students that they all, as a team, are responsible for predicting, clarifying, questioning, and summarizing— as is needed. They are instructed to implement these tasks whenever appropriate in a context that creates a conversation. Anyone in the group, at this point, can do any of the jobs. What occurs as a result is a thoughtful, in-depth conversation about text—exactly what Mr. Davidson wants from his student groups. To facilitate an understanding of what each of the tasks entails, Mr. Davidson provides students with cue cards that have prompts to stimulate thinking (Figure 4.3).

Figure 4.3   Reciprocal Teaching Cue Cards

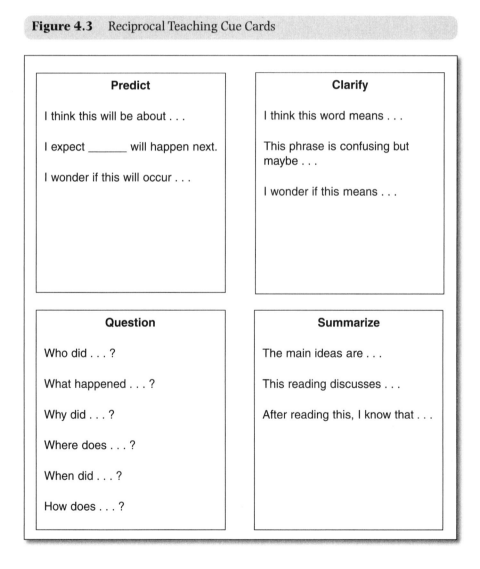

INCORPORATING INDEPENDENT PRACTICE

Independent work is a critical step toward the ultimate goal of becoming an independent science reader and learner. Mr. Davidson chose to implement an independent practice activity after his students completed the Reciprocal Teaching reading. For this assignment, he asked his students to read the textbook chapters that dealt with ionic and covalent bonds while completing a double entry note-taking guide. For students who might benefit from more scaffolding, Mr. Davidson provided a note-taking template that meshed with the textbook pages that were assigned (Figure 4.4). Students who were more advanced in terms of note-taking could develop their own guide. While it may at first seem logical to move from focus lessons to guided practice and onto collaborative learning and independent practice, there may be times, especially in a science class, where a teacher will want students to tackle independent work at the start of a lesson.

Figure 4.4   Sample Note-Taking Page

Main Ideas/Questions	Details/Answers
What is an ionic bond?	
Which elements will most likely form ionic bonds?	
How do covalent bonds form?	
Which elements will form covalent bonds?	
Explain the chart on page 124.	
Summary (Write two or three sentences that describe the main ideas of this reading.)	

Teacher Cindy Woo teaches a unit in which she addresses the standard that asks students to investigate a science-based societal issue by researching the literature, analyzing data, and communicating the findings (California Department of Education, 2002). She begins by having her students read an article about the first successful cloning of a common house cat. The reading is at a suitable reading level for all students in the class and is intended to generate interest in a current societal issue—the issue of cloning.

In science, disciplinary literacy often involves collaborative discussions and the construction of content-based background knowledge *before* individual efforts are put into play. A science research team will commonly sit down for a hashing out of ideas, many times founded in referenced research from the literature, before dividing up individual tasks. By mixing up the elements of the Fisher and Frey instructional protocol, a teacher may allow students to more closely approximate the methods of inquiry conducted by scientists.

Students are asked to read the article independently. From this assignment, Ms. Woo moves to a collaborative reading activity in which students, in groups of four, read two articles—one written from the perspective of a proponent of cloning and one from an opposition view. The students use Reciprocal Teaching to dissect and discuss the articles. Following this, Ms. Woo models how to read one of these same two articles, both opinion articles, in a critical manner. She presents issues of credibility, referencing, and documentation of information, all key elements of disciplinary science reading. Next, using the second article, Ms. Woo rehearses with students using the method of critiquing that she modeled. She does this in a guided practice format. Clearly Ms. Woo has found a way to implement Fisher and Frey's instructional protocol (2008a) in an investigative and inquiry-based manner. She lets students inspect the content and then models and practices how to evaluate it.

WHY TEACH READING IN SCIENCE?

A major intent of any science curriculum is to promote science literacy. To be scientifically literate, a person must be able to read and understand a variety of science texts so that he or she can thoughtfully engage in meaningful conversations about science issues (Sanders et al., 2007). Reading in science can be different than reading in other content areas. The unique text structures, vocabulary, and presentation of informational content need to be explored within the constructs of an instructional protocol. With this thought in mind, reading can be and should often be a social process that involves the construction of meaning through dialogue (Donahue, 2000). By allowing students to see and hear how to read using read-alouds, shared readings, and think-alouds, they are better able to build vocabulary, access prior knowledge, and fill in gaps in background knowledge. Additionally, opportunities for both collaborative and independent reading will help students become scientifically literate people that are informed about science issues and are able to articulate ideas and opinions about relevant topics.

Writing in Science   **5**

Scaffolding Skills for
Science Students

Miguel Mejia is a bench scientist in Los Angeles. He spends a significant part of his day setting up and executing laboratory investigations for a Southern California biotechnology company. When Miguel applied for this position, his employer, in addition to reviewing Miguel's resume and references, asked for a writing sample. Miguel's employer did not ask for an essay or a literary paragraph but an example of writing that demonstrated Miguel's ability to succinctly and accurately report lab findings. In essence, the hiring manager wanted to see if Miguel could write like a scientist.

As a student in high school, Miguel first learned to write like a scientist when his eleventh-grade teacher asked him for a formal laboratory report. The development of the report entailed conducting research, gathering and recording data, and then finally composing the required report. To be successful, Miguel had to incorporate key vocabulary terms, develop a concise and to-the-point phrasing, and use a logical format. While the means by which Miguel's teacher could get his students to compose a well-written report may seem simple, it is in actuality quite intricate. It requires more than just the delivery of information—more than a handout that presents the correct form of the familiar scientific method. Miguel's teacher needed to do the following: model how to formulate and record a hypothesis or prediction, share the various ways to present data, explore the differences between expository and narrative writing, and demonstrate the thinking that goes into analyzing and drawing conclusions by evaluating results. It's not enough to tell students to do these things when they write. Teaching students to write like a scientist requires a period in which students observe as the teacher models. This needs to be followed by instruction that offers scaffolding for the required skills in an environment that includes practice of these skills. Finally, students need to have opportunities to independently use the newly learned science writing skills.

What makes writing like a scientist different from writing like a historian or a mathematician? How can teachers help students write within a science context? Is it important for students studying science to learn to write like a scientist? These questions are at the heart of the writing issue. They are questions that beg to be examined in further detail.

WRITING LIKE A SCIENTIST IS DIFFERENT

Most of us are familiar with the connections that exist between math and science. It's an undeniable fact that physics will forever be associated with the algebraic calculations of $F = ma$. There is, however, more to the language of science than simply balancing equations, calculating molar concentrations, and determining momentum. Science involves the communication of ideas via written language for numerous important reasons, including (Yore, Hand, & Florence, 2004) the following:

- Establishing detailed associations among evidence, warrants, claims, and reflective commentary
- Developing and conveying mental images
- Expressing ownership of intellectual properties

In order for scientists to become active members of the scientific community, they must have well-developed print-based language skills (Yore, Florence, Pearson, & Weaver, 2006). Learning to write like a scientist involves the integration of certain tasks, especially those involving language and instruction, into inquiry activities (Yore, 2000).

To determine how teachers can best scaffold learning to ensure that students become proficient science writers, it's important to consider the components that comprise scientific literacy. To be scientifically literate, a person must have an understanding of the nature of science and inquiry, along with a working knowledge of the function of reasoning and interpretive beliefs (Hand, Lawrence, Prain, & Yore, 1999). It's clear that science literacy involves evaluation, debate, and explanation. It's more than merely knowing how to follow the aforementioned scientific method—a strategy for scientific inquiry that is typically presented at the start of each school year in a fashion that is rote, tedious, and by nature of the repetition of its presentation, usually boring.

To help students comprehend the nature of science in a way that allows them to be able to write about the content, teachers need to present problem-based activities that allow collaboration, discussion, and the generation of ideas. Such activities will provide students with material from which they may compose science-based writings. Hug, Krajcik, and Marx (2005) suggest offering project-based activities that incorporate innovative learning technologies such as the use of the Internet, probes, modeling tools, and visualization software. Such activities prompt students to ask more meaningful and worthwhile questions and guide them as they find new information.

With this kind of foundation, students will have material from which they may extract content for science writing. Clearly, a writer of science must be able to ask questions, seek out answers, and make connections to other knowledge. An environment that promotes inquiry sets the stage for science writing.

--------------------------- ⚬⚬ ---------------------------

WEBQUEST: COLLECTING DATA TO WRITE

As with any genre, a writer needs experiences from which he or she can draw ideas to formulate text material. There are many types of experiences that can offer material from which science authorship can emanate. For example, a WebQuest activity that promotes questioning, data collection and data analysis, along with problem solving would lay the groundwork for a student to write in a science format. This is the stimulus that's needed to support the development of science writing proficiency (see www.webquest.org).

Building off of the idea that science writers compose writing that incorporates referenced background knowledge, presents questions, and provides documentation of research and related conclusions, a teacher must consider the following when scaffolding these disciplinary literacy skills: students' construction of background knowledge and the ability to reference it, use of technical and academic vocabulary common to science writing, and flow or structure of written text. Certain ways of *flowing*, like problem-data-solution, are more common in science writing.

A WebQuest is an inquiry-oriented lesson format in which most or all of the information learners work with comes from the Web (Dodge, 2007). A WebQuest is just one of the many types of activities that incorporate relevant, current issues in a project-based form. Students involved in project-based science courses that focus on real-world issues have demonstrated an ability to perform on achievement tests as well or better than similar student populations involved in traditional science programs (Schneider, Krajcik, Marx, & Soloway, 2002).

In addition to having research-based material to write about, students need to have knowledge of science-based ideas to which they can connect their own ideas. On a scholarly level, this is known as intertextuality (Chaopricha, 1997). While it's not expected that high school or middle school students read the latest scholarly journal, it is probable that students will be exposed to the work and ideas developed by Newton, Einstein, Bohr, Curie, and others that contributed in major ways to our grand body of science knowledge. It is with this work as a foundation that students can build ideas in written form and do so as writers of science.

Imagine now that the students in Ms. Williams' ninth-grade Earth science class have an understanding of Alfred Wegener's continental drift idea and about the sea-floor spreading theory developed by Harry Hess and R. Deitz. They've worked with animated models of plates on computer screens and have collaborated in teams to use magnetic anomalies to calculate spreading rates. In essence, the students have studied the most relevant work of researchers in this field and have engaged in problem-based activities. Given this, we have to ask whether every student is ready to respond in writing to a prompt that asks them to relate the history and development of the theory of plate tectonics. Most likely, even some of the most diligent students will not be able to respond to such a prompt.

Sandra, an eager, hardworking, ninth grader, sits with a blank paper on her desk, twirling her pencil as she flips through the pages of Chapter 5 in her text. It's clear that Sandra, an active participant in labs and an avid reader in science class, is still unable to begin. Perhaps for some students, there is still something missing. Are there ways for teachers to help students like Sandra, students who have the information they need and who have been engaged in meaningful science activities?

WRITING FRAMES: SCAFFOLDS
FOR SCIENTIFIC WRITING

One of the most difficult aspects of the writing process is knowing where to start. A science teacher can help a student with this task by providing sentence starters and paragraph frames. Sentence starters are writing frames that provide writers with phrases that connect to the topic to be explored and act as a means of framing a written response to a question or prompt. Sandra might have been able to respond to the plate tectonics prompt if Ms. Williams had provided her with the following sentence starter: The theory of plate tectonics, which originated in the 1960s as an outgrowth of Wegener's continental drift idea, helped to explain _____.

Such a sentence starter could provide students with a topic sentence that would serve as a springboard for continued writing. For students that need further scaffolding, Ms. Williams could provide a sentence starter for each ensuing paragraph. For example, if the previously mentioned sentence starter began the response, the following sentence starter could provide guidance as the student begins the second paragraph: Alfred Wegener identified three types of evidence to support his theory, including _____. The third paragraph might start with this: The theory of plate tectonics differed from the idea of continental drift because _____. A concluding paragraph could start with this: Plate tectonics theory currently helps scientists to explain various features seen on earth including _____.

So as not to neglect the ever-present laboratory write-up—the staple of most science classrooms—consider the use of sentence starters to scaffold the lab report. Many teachers already provide headings for students to use: *problem, hypothesis, data, analysis,* and *conclusion.* For some students, more support may be needed. For example, a data analysis section could have the following sentence starters:

My data shows that over time bacteria _____.

The evidence for this is _____.

Based on this evidence, I determine that _____.

Especially when students are just learning how to connect data to concluding ideas, a structured framework can be very helpful.

Sentence starters provided in this fashion guide students in terms of organization and logical structure. Additionally, they help to trigger recall of information learned. As students become more familiar with organizing science paragraphs, the sentence starter scaffold can be reduced and eventually eliminated in a way that provides a gradual release of responsibility (Pearson & Gallagher, 1983).

It is important at this point to remember that vocabulary knowledge, treated in extensive detail in Chapter 3, is an underpinning of scientific writing. In addition to developing word knowledge as a foundational tool to effective science writing, it is important for writers to be able to organize content in a logical and sophisticated manner. One way to scaffold this skill is to integrate the use of graphic organizers into the science curriculum.

Certain graphic organizers are more appropriate for certain kinds of content. For example, a *flow chart* is a suitable choice for material that involves the steps to a process or a sequence of events (Figure 5.1). A student that is describing the steps to solve a freefall problem might organize his or her ideas using this type of graphic organizer. *Cycle* graphic organizers are appropriate for use with science concepts like the water cycle or the rock cycle. Ideas that involve a hierarchy may use a *tree* format. Topics dealing with taxonomy are appropriately organized in a hierarchical format.

Figure 5.1   Flow Chart, Cycle Chart, and Tree Format

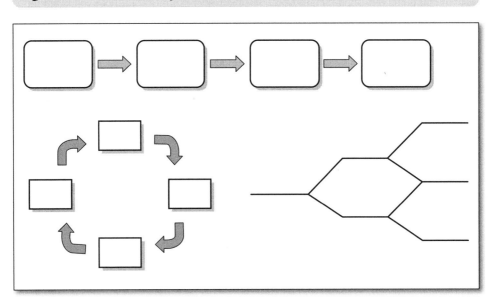

TEACHING SCIENTIFIC PHRASING

Imagine reading a science-related paragraph that possessed long, complex sentences. Here is an example:

> Plant cells, which typically have strong cell walls, take up water by osmosis and swell, but they are prevented from rupture by the aforementioned cell wall. In dilute solutions, plant cells become turgid, or hard and distended, because the pressure inside the cell increases to the point at which it is completely saturated with water, leaving no more room for any additional fluid. This hydrostatic pressure works in opposition to osmosis, and the turgidity results in the rigidity of the green parts of plants when they are exposed to the sun's light.

Could you decipher meaning easily and without frustration? If you were somewhat familiar with the complex phrasing that is characteristic of some science writing, you probably had an easier time.

Now imagine that you're a 13-year-old or 14-year-old and your perceived idea of *writing like a scientist* involves the generation of long, intricate sentences, loaded with technical terms that would confuse all but the best-trained science reader. If this is your idea of science writing, how would you feel if confronted with the task of writing a science paragraph? While clearly not every student feels that writing like a scientist requires complicated phrasing, many do hold the belief that science writing is dry and packed with long sentences that traverse pages monotonously. By many people, science writing is considered difficult to comprehend. To the end of removing this stigma, science teachers can show students that there are ways to create readable science texts.

Science writing is succinct and often loaded with properties, data, and evidence. To support disciplinary literacy growth, a teacher might guide students to employ a list format that states steps, properties, data, and evidence in a numbered fashion. Teaching students to reference their data tables and graphs in their writing is also critical to supporting focused science writing. Both of these elements mirror the writing style used by many science writers.

Maxine Warren, a veteran teacher, offers her tenth-grade biology students a wide array of experiences to help them understand the process of osmosis. In addition to doing a shared reading with the textbook, Mrs. Warren asks her students to work in laboratory groups to complete an experiment using dialysis tubing and glucose or starch solutions of various concentrations. Like any attentive lab teacher, Mrs. Warren moves around the classroom, visiting lab groups in order to monitor progress. When asked about the lab results and the data, Charlene seems to understand that the net movement of water across this selectively permeable membrane is driven by a difference in solute concentrations on the two sides of the membrane. Even though she can orally respond to queries in an accurate and meaningful manner, Charlene has trouble documenting her results in written form. To help Charlene and the many other students who struggle with this, Mrs. Warren has presented a means by which students can summarize and explain results in a clear, concise manner. First, she starts with one of the biggest roadblocks, *phrasing.* Mrs. Warren has shown students that science writing does not have to consist of a long series of compound sentences strung together. Instead, she has suggested that her students incorporate simple sentences of varying length. The paragraph shown earlier could be rewritten as follows:

> Plant cells have strong cell walls. When plant cells take up water by osmosis and swell, the cell wall prevents them from bursting. In dilute solutions, plant cells become turgid, or hard and distended. The pressure inside the cell increases to the point at which it is completely full with water. This hydrostatic pressure works against osmosis. The turgidity causes the stiffness seen in the green parts of plants when they are exposed to the sun's light.

According to Kirkman (2005), readable science writing not only entails the use of simple, yet varied sentences, but it often employs sub-clauses, a means of clarifying and making text understandable. Another version of the aforementioned paragraph could read as follows:

Plant cells have strong cell walls. Here's how osmosis works in a plant cell:

1. Plant cells take up water and swell.
2. The strength of the cell wall prevents them from bursting.
3. In dilute solutions, plant cells become turgid, or hard and distended.
4. Also in dilute solutions, the pressure inside the plant cell increases to the point at which it is completely full with water.
5. At this point, hydrostatic pressure works against osmosis.
6. The turgidity causes the stiffness seen in the green parts of plants when they are exposed to the sun's light.

While there is no single "right way" to phrase a paragraph like the one shown earlier, the latter two versions are more approachable for the novice science writer and for those learning new content. When students are exposed to the various ways they can formally write science content, they become increasingly more comfortable with undertaking a writing task themselves.

WRITING FORMATS IN SCIENCE

Prain and Hand (1996) suggest that writing in science can extend beyond the formal laboratory write-up and can be used as a resource for thinking and learning. In essence, writing in science should not be exclusively reserved for explaining experimental findings. It should also be incorporated as a means to clarify and consolidate information—a way to make science more accessible, humanistic, and personal. Many well-known, highly regarded scientists, including Galileo and da Vinci, are revered for their personal and thoughtful science journaling.

Writing to learn is an instructional routine that allows students to negotiate their own learning in a

---

It is common practice for science writers to explore ideas in an informal manner. Most scientists in the field record notes and ideas by scribbling in notebooks or journals when a thought strikes them. Leonardo da Vinci's margin notes and journal entries provide evidence enough that scientists need opportunities to informally document ideas. Journal writing is clearly a means by which to move students through basic literacy into intermediate and disciplinary literacy.

constructivist, student-centered manner using their own language to learn science (Prain & Hand, 1996). Writing for the purpose of learning can create a place for experimentation. Jenkinson (1988) suggests that student writers explore subjects, examine their own feelings about a topic, and solve problems through writing. Students can benefit from being encouraged to practice writing without the omnipresent fear of a red marking pen slashing lines through misspelled words and around errors in grammar and missing punctuation marks. Writing to learn is an instructional routine that promotes writing without the usual penalties mentioned in the previous sentence. Students that are given opportunities to practice writing in a supportive environment are more likely to get better at the task. Yore, Hand, and Prain (1999) developed a template for the Science Writing Heuristic (SWH), a method that encourages learners to discover solutions for themselves. The SWH asks students to predict, revisit, and reflect on learning and ideas. It could easily be used as guide for journal writing that is incorporated as a companion to laboratory investigation (see Figure 5.2).

To support students as they explore predictions, sort out understandings, interpret ideas, and revisit new learnings, a teacher must provide student writers with a sense of purpose and a target audience. Simply speaking, to successfully write about science, students need a topic, an indication of the type of writing intended, a purpose for writing, an audience for which the writing is intended, and a method in which the text is produced (Hand & Prain, 1996). Carmen Segovia offers the following

Figure 5.2   The Science Writing Heuristic Template for Student Thinking

1. Beginning Ideas—What are my questions?

2. Tests—What did I do?

3. Observations—What did I see?

4. Claims—What can I claim?

5. Evidence—How do I know?

   Why am I making these claims?

6. Reading—How do my ideas compare with others?

7. Reflection—How have my ideas changed?

SOURCE: Yore, L. D., Hand, B., & Prain, V. (1999). *Writing to learn science: Breakthroughs, barriers, and promises.* Paper presented at the International Conference of the Association for Educating Teachers in Science.

instructions to her eleventh- and twelfth-grade physics students who had just learned about sound waves and acoustics, including the concepts related to reflection, echoes, and reverberation:

> Your task is to develop a *diagram* of an auditorium, theater, or concert hall that will provide *optimum acoustics* for a musical performance. You must also include a *written report* that *explains your devised plan.* Your diagram and report are intended for a *community board* that will *evaluate your ideas.* You should develop this plan *with a partner using a computer or pencil/paper.*

Notice that Miss Segovia indicates that the topic is *optimum acoustics,* the type of writing is a *diagram* and an accompanying *written report that explains the devised plan,* the purpose is for a group of people to *evaluate ideas,* the audience is *a community board,* and the method in which the text may be produced is with a *partner using a computer or with pencil/paper.* Students are given information and structure, yet they have the freedom to construct, negotiate, evaluate, and reevaluate their own ideas.

Another way to help students build their own knowledge is to have them participate in perspective writing using the RAFT writing prompt. RAFT stands for the following:

R = Role (Who is the writer?)

A = Audience (To whom is the writer writing?)

F = Format (What format is used for the writing?)

T = Topic (What are you writing about?)

Claude Maxwell, an eighth-grade physical science teacher, uses RAFT to guide students to revisit a newly studied topic. For example, after learning about Newton's Universal Law of Gravitation, Mr. Maxwell asked his third-period class to write using the following RAFT prompt:

R = an apple

A = planet Earth

F = a telegram

T = I'm falling for you

As seen in Figure 5.3, Chloe, a student in Mr. Maxwell's class, wrote about the distance of her small apple from planet earth and about the strength of the attraction of massive planet earth. She described how the pull of gravity was greater as the distance between her (the apple) and earth decreased. Her response to the RAFT was exactly what Mr. Maxwell had hoped for. Chloe explored the newly learned relationships between the force of gravity, the mass of the two objects, and the distance between the objects. She did so without the apprehension that is sometimes generated by a more formal writing experience. A RAFT provides structure and guidance but typically offers a context that is approachable and relevant. Occasionally, Mr. Maxwell has his students develop their own RAFTs for a given topic, as can be seen in Figure 5.4.

Figure 5.3 Student Writing in Response to a RAFT prompt

Message to Earth – I am an apple and I'm very attracted to you by a special force known as gravity. You have made me fall from my branch. The closer I fall to you, the more you pull on me. By the time you get this telegram I'll probly be sitting on your grass.

Figure 5.4 Student-Generated RAFT Prompts

R = Grass	R = Hydrogen
A = Dew	A = Oxygen
F = Diary	F = Memo
T = How I hold you	T = Let's make water
R = Mosquito	R = Brain
A = Human snack	A = Muscle
F = Cartoon	F = Letter of request
T = My bite is bad	T = Move

WHY LEARN TO WRITE LIKE A SCIENTIST?

Many careers opportunities are available to young people interested in science, health, and engineering. All of these fields require specific knowledge of content, an understanding of methods of inquiry, knowledge and understanding of content-specific terms and academic vocabulary, and a means of developing structure and organization for science concepts. These are the underpinnings of clear, precise science writing. Given the doors of opportunity that open to students who have mastered these skills, it is imperative that teachers of biology, chemistry, physics, Earth science, and other science-related fields, integrate instruction that includes strategies related to problem-based learning, the acquisition of background knowledge, vocabulary development, graphic organization, and structure and form. It is equally essential that Language Arts teachers encourage students to read scientific informational books and write informational reports. It is through the use of such strategies that students will develop the ability to effectively write, not like a mathematician or a historian, but like a scientist.

Assessing Student   **6**
 Learning in Science

The interest in science assessment and science instruction has been heightened in recent years by the very public comparisons between students in the United States and science students in other countries using measures like the Trends in International Mathematics and Science Study (TIMSS, n.d.). While the 2003 data shows that U.S. fourth graders exceeded international averages in both math and science (National Center for Education Statistics), it also shows that students in Chinese Taipei, Japan, and Singapore were able to outperform U.S. students. This implies that there is room for improvement in terms of science instruction and the resultant student construction of content knowledge. The TIMSS also highlights the need for frequent monitoring of progress. Teachers clearly need to check in with students frequently to see if what they intend to teach is really being taught.

THE PURPOSE OF ASSESSMENT IN SCIENCE

It's useful to look at assessment from two perspectives:

1. Assessment as a way to determine whether the planned lessons are meeting students needs.

2. Assessment as a way to measure individual student progress toward predetermined goals and objectives.

Let's examine each of these purposes for assessment.

Patricia Valencia teaches ninth-grade Earth science. She uses small-scale, frequently administered, informal assessments as a way to gauge the strengths and weaknesses of her instructional methodologies. In an attempt to help her students understand that air exerts pressure and that this results in various weather patterns, she employed a demonstration she has seen several times on reruns of the old Mr. Wizard television show. She carefully prepared for a smooth execution of the demonstration by hard-boiling an egg, having a glass juice jar with a medium-wide mouth at hand, and setting out a beaker of water to which she would toss in burnt matches after she lit a piece of newspaper. Mrs. Valencia called for a volunteer to peel the shell off the hard-boiled egg and told the student to place it onto the mouth of the jar right after a piece of burning newspaper was placed in the jar. All went smoothly and the egg slipped almost effortlessly into the jar. As student applause subsided, Mrs. Valencia did her best to explain how the pressure was lowered in the jar as the paper burned. "The higher pressure of the air outside of the jar pushed the egg into the jar," she said.

When it came time to assess the students' understanding, Mrs. Valencia decided she should ask the students to write a short paragraph in which they explained how the demonstration relates to air pressure and weather. This was a spur-of-the-moment decision, but it turned out to be valuable. Because in a previous lesson, Mrs. Valencia had discussed high pressure and low pressure systems, she expected students to be able to make connections between content presented across these lessons. After school, she reviewed the student paragraphs.

To her disappointment, students, while engaged and interested in the demonstration, did not make the expected connections between air pressure and weather. Randy, one of Mrs. Valencia's most eager students, wrote this: "The fire caused the air to pull the egg into the jar. Maybe this is similar to the force that pulls a tornado around in a cone shape." As Mrs. Valencia leafed through each paper, it became clear that no one could connect the dots between the demonstration, air pressure, and resultant weather phenomenon. Mrs. Valencia could have been like so many other educators who express thoughts like these: *students today just aren't like those of the past* or *I know I explained it, but they just didn't get it.* Instead, she came to the realization that she herself needed to rethink the instruction of the concepts that were being taught.

Instead of laying the blame on the students, Mrs. Valencia used her informal assessment to evaluate her instruction. Since no students made the expected connections, something clearly went wrong in the delivery of information. To facilitate a better understanding of the problem, Mrs. Valencia scheduled a lunch meeting with a colleague who also taught ninth-grade Earth science. She carefully described her demonstration and her egg-air pressure explanation to Miss Davis, a 10-year veteran of Earth science instruction. As the conversation progressed, it became clear that students needed more background knowledge regarding high and low air pressure systems and the resultant weather phenomenon. The teacher pair also decided that it would be helpful to allow students to work with a partner to figure out how the egg moved into the jar. The students needed more opportunity to build their own ideas through reading and conversations with peers. In this instance, assessment wasn't for the purpose of awarding grades. It was, in fact, a tool to dissect instructional methods in order to build a more effective lesson.

Good assessment can be a mechanism to improve curriculum and instruction. To contrast, poor assessment can hinder science instruction by focusing teachers and students on efforts that are minor or on test taking as merely an endpoint (Stern & Ahlgren, 2002). Well-crafted assessments can provide information about each student's understanding of the content. By employing a formal or informal data analysis methodology, teachers can use assessment information to make decisions about instruction, interventions, and reteaching (Fisher & Frey, 2007).

In the aforementioned example, Mrs. Valencia used an informal assessment technique in which students were asked to explain, in written form, phenomena that they observed and read about. Mrs. Valencia did not require a prescribed writing structure with drafts and rewrites. She instead wanted students to think about what they knew and what they had just learned for the purpose of making connections. While in this instance, students were unable to satisfactorily accomplish the task and after analysis of the situation, Mrs. Valencia concluded that a different instructional path should be fol-

> Scientists informally and formally revisit data so that they can make decisions about next steps. This is done often throughout a research project. Given this, a teacher might consider making her formative assessments very transparent, revealing data collected, conclusions about instruction, and next steps to the students. Because this is a common practice of scientists, it helps students achieve more in the way of disciplinary literacy.

lowed, she did come away with valuable information—information that guided her decisions about the next steps to take. What Mrs. Valencia was conducting is called *formative assessment.*

Formative assessment may be defined as assessment *for* learning, not assessment *of* learning (Black, 1993; Ruiz-Primo & Furtak, 2006). Within the context of formative assessment, there is a continuum between formal and informal gathering of student data. Formal formative assessments are designed by the teacher, in advance of instruction. They may be in the form of quizzes, responses to questions, project activities, or any number of assessment methods. Any assessment that is specifically designed in advance to provide information on student learning so that levels of student understanding may be determined and next steps may be taken is a formal formative assessment. To contrast, an informal formative assessment is more impromptu—students participate in a learning activity and the teacher regularly checks in, at points determined during the teaching process, to see who's acquiring an understanding of the content (Ruiz-Primo & Furtak, 2006). Given this understanding of formative assessment, how can a teacher determine the success of the instruction?

USING ASSESSMENT INFORMATION

In science, assessment and content instruction often go hand in hand. For example, when a science teacher asks students to work with their peers to solve a laboratory problem, content discussions, centered on the data and corresponding analysis, are expected. If a teacher circulates around the room and listens in on these conversations, he or she has the opportunity to informally engage in formative assessment. Based on student conversations, decisions can be made about upcoming instruction. If many students are struggling with content, the teacher may determine a means by which students may review key ideas. If only a few are in need of support, an intervention may be developed. If all students are demonstrating an understanding, the teacher may move forward with more challenging content. An effective teacher makes such decisions several times during the course of a class period.

As was previously mentioned, not only can assessment be used for gaining insight into what is working in terms of instruction, but it may also be used for diagnosing who is understanding presented content, who needs a little more support, and who is really struggling. By having frequent checkpoints for assessment, a teacher is better able to pinpoint where problems might be occurring for individual students. Likewise, he or she will be able to see who needs more challenges because they have extensive background knowledge, they are easily accessing content, or both. A student who is bored because he or she is reviewing already-learned content needs as much attention as a struggling student. In today's classrooms, teachers, on a daily basis, encounter large numbers of students with a wide array of needs. Well-crafted assessments can be the key to providing the individualized attention that students and parents are rightfully demanding.

There are many ways that a teacher can incorporate informal formative assessment so that it drives instruction and student learning. Figure 6.1 provides a template for thinking about the data that informal assessment provides to a teacher. When using assessment to determine if instruction is effective, look at the overall achievement of the class. If, in general, students are *not* ready to move on after new content is presented, the teacher may need to rethink the instruction. Effective instruction will meet the needs of most students, even if those needs are wide and diverse. If most or all students are ready to move on to new content, and only a few need more support or more challenges, the instruction may be considered effective. If the majority of students need more challenges, the instruction needs revision. In essence, to evaluate instructional methodologies, look at the achievement of the class as a whole. Because the success of the class as whole depends on the understanding of individuals, it's also critical to look at the needs of individuals. The last two columns of Figure 6.1 are for teachers to note who needs more support and who needs more challenges. After looking at this general achievement of the class and students, it's time to pinpoint what specifically students need to be challenged and successful.

Figure 6.1 Type of Formative Assessment

Formative Assessment					
	Overall Assessment of Class Achievement			Individual Needs to Be Addressed	
Informal	Not ready to move on	Ready to move on to next concepts	Need more challenging content	Students in need of extra support	Students in need of more challenges
Laboratory discussions					
Graphic organizers					
Partner or group talk about readings or lectures					
Questioning (QAR, ReQuest, Reciprocal Teaching)					
Writing activities					
Other instructional activities used by the teacher					

IDENTIFYING SPECIFIC STUDENTS' NEEDS

There are certain aspects of assessment that fit specifically with science instruction. As has been mentioned in previous chapters, vocabulary and background knowledge are essential to content understanding. We have focused on these areas and how they fit with reading and writing in science. How then can a science teacher assess these aspects of science learning that are so critical to thinking and expressing ideas in science? Perhaps one of the best ways to look at this issue is to break up assessment into the following component parts: oral language, written language, and content knowledge. Within these component parts, specific areas of achievement can be evaluated. Figure 6.2 presents criteria that could be used to evaluate these narrowed areas of science learning. While these criteria only represent a sample of the component parts that a teacher might want to assess, they are areas to begin looking at in terms of evaluation.

To be scientifically literate, one must be able to participate in conversations that are founded in an ability to read and understand science texts (Sanders et al., 2007). Consequently, if one of the goals of teachers is to create a cadre of scientifically literate students, we must make the teaching and practice of oral language in science a part of the curriculum, and we must assess students to determine if related goals are being meet. Oral language has two component parts: speaking and listening (Cooper & Moreale, 2003; Fisher & Frey, 2007). Within the context of an English class, speech is commonly taught, but *science talk*—and the requirements that make for proficient science talk—are often ignored as a topic of instruction. ReQuest and Reciprocal Teaching are excellent frames for generating science conversations, but how might a teacher assess the speaking aspects of science talk?

As discussed in previous chapters, an understanding and ability to use both appropriate academic and technical terms in science is an underpinning of the ability to acquire and access content knowledge. Use of vocabulary should be a focus of oral language assessment. If vocabulary knowledge is present, then the next component to evaluate is the ability to make connections between science ideas. These might be connections made between prior and new content ideas or they might be connections between several newly

---
❦

To determine whether students are acquiring disciplinary literacy skills, assessment should be focused on oral language, written language, and content knowledge. The last of these, content knowledge, is typically the focus of science instruction. While it is critical, it is not the only element that needs to be evaluated when considering the acquisition of disciplinary literacy. Scientists always express themselves both orally and in writing.

Figure 6.2 Assessment Using Oral Language, Written Language, and Content Knowledge

Levels of Achievement	Not Yet Proficient	Nearly Proficient	Proficient	Highly Proficient
Oral Language				
• Speaking				
Uses academic and technical vocabulary				
Makes connections between content ideas				
Uses appropriate grammar				
Presents a logical flow of ideas				
• Listening				
Asks clarifying questions				
Interprets speaker's ideas				
Paraphrases speaker's ideas				
Analyzes speaker's ideas				
Written Language				
Uses academic and technical vocabulary				
Makes connections between content ideas				
Uses appropriate grammar				
Presents a logical flow of ideas				
Content Knowledge				
Possesses accurate information				
Understands connections between conceptual ideas				
Understands theoretical information				
Understands practical information and relevant applications of science concepts				

learned concepts. When assessing use of grammar in science, in addition to the usual sentence structure expectations, a teacher should look for students using some of the more common science text structures, including description, problem/solution, compare/contrast, cause/effect, and sequencing. Last, spoken language in science needs to have a logical flow that is dependent on the topic to be presented. For example, if a student is presenting information about the science of motors, he or she might use a description text structure with appropriate physics terms and a logical flow that includes information about the construction of a motor, the physics behind motors, and the uses of motors.

Listening is an equally important aspect of oral language. Listening involves asking clarifying questions when needed, finding ways to interpret a speaker's ideas, having an ability to paraphrase ideas, and analyzing heard concepts. These aspects of listening are critical to any collaboration, and collaboration is the foundation of most science efforts throughout the world. When Al Gore gave his Nobel Peace Prize lecture in Oslo on December 10, 2007, he began by acknowledging his colleagues in science—those who have laid the foundation for understanding the problem of global warming that we face today (http://nobelprize.org/nobel_prizes/peace/laureates/2007/press.html).

The prestigious award was given to Al Gore and to the Intergovernmental Panel on Climate Change—a collaborative effort that would not have come to fruition were it not for those involved having the expert ability to listen and interpret information. Clearly oral language skills are critical for the construction and use of science knowledge in any local, statewide, or global effort. Teachers must support students to acquire these incredibly valuable skills. Instructional routines like Reciprocal Teaching and ReQuest require that students listen, question, and interpret information in a collegial, collaborative way. We must build in assessments that evaluate the achievement of such oral language skills.

Science ideas are not only generated through oral language; they are also expressed in writing. Attention to the evaluation of writing skills in science is equally important. Because both oral and written expressions are ways of communicating science information, the criteria for evaluation of each are similar. Again, the use of appropriate academic and technical vocabulary is foundational. Evaluation of science writing should examine a student's ability to make connections between ideas, use proper grammar and text structures, and present information that flows logically and smoothly.

Finally, let's look at what most teachers, school districts, and parents are concerned with when they think of assessment: science content. High-stakes state tests have been established to evaluate content knowledge; therefore, it is clearly on the minds of all educators and at the forefront of most science reform efforts. To address this, we suggest that teachers look at the following aspects of content knowledge when evaluating students: possesses accurate information, understands connections between conceptual ideas, understands theoretical information, and understands practical information and relevant applications of science concepts. The specific type of information and connections are, of course, dependent on the content being taught. Figure 6.3 shows a modified version of a piece of the assessment table, specifically designed for reviewing Mrs. Valencia's writing activity.

Figure 6.3 Assessment of Writing in Science

Levels of Achievement	Not Yet Proficient	Nearly Proficient	Proficient	Highly Proficient
Written Language				
Uses academic and technical vocabulary: high pressure, low pressure, air pressure at sea level (14.7 psi), precipitation, fair weather				
Makes connections between content ideas: low-pressure systems are associated with clouds and precipitation; high-pressure systems are associated with fair weather and clear skies; the demo showed a change in air pressure in the jar—from higher pressure to lower pressure after the paper was burned. Higher pressure outside the jar pushed the egg into the jar. Air moves from areas of high pressure to areas of low pressure, thus causing winds.				
Uses appropriate grammar—look for cause-and-effect text structures				
Presents a logical flow of ideas—includes explanation of demo and connection to wind				

CREATING SCIENCE ASSESSMENTS

We've looked at what areas of learning should be assessed; now it's time to examine how assessments may be created. If assessments need to serve two purposes—(1) that of providing feedback regarding instruction and (2) that of providing information on individual student accomplishments—then the creation of high-quality assessments is vital. The value of any assessment data is dependent upon the quality of the assessment itself. For example, the common multiple-choice assessment, while convenient, quick, and easy to score, is typically used to assess nothing more than rote memorization of basic science facts (Stern & Ahlgren, 2002). In such a case, the data would only provide information about basic content knowledge. In an example of this, Stern and Ahlgren (2002) note the following:

> Regarding the topic "processes that shape the earth," students are asked many questions that require the knowledge of excruciating details related to the mechanisms of individual processes that shape the earth, but rarely are they asked about the impact of these processes on the continually changing surface of the earth. (p. 906)

According to Klassen (2006), learning is a sensemaking activity in which the learner fits new information to existing mental structures. What if, then, a teacher wants to go beyond the basic knowledge level and desires to assess higher-order thinking, including the analysis and synthesis of ideas?

Creating assessments that provide information about students' understandings requires teacher collaboration and the analysis of student data. It is a recursive process that entails review and occasional revision. The aforementioned multiple-choice test—which has too often been relegated to assessing *only* basic knowledge—can be written in a way that taps into the higher-order realms of thinking. To start, teachers can begin with prompts that tie to the various levels of Bloom's Taxonomy (Bloom, 1956). The levels of competence described by Bloom are as follows:

Level 1—Knowledge: knowing facts, figures, and simple processes

Level 2—Comprehension: showing an understanding of facts and information

Level 3—Application: generalizing the facts to fit other situations

Level 4—Analysis: showing an understanding of the components of facts and information

Level 5—Synthesis: making connections between information pieces

Level 6—Evaluation: using knowledge to determine and establish the value of information

Figure 6.4 contains a list of terms that help teachers develop question prompts to address various levels of thinking. Specifically, choice questions can be written with the intent of moving into the higher levels, particularly Levels 4, 5, and 6. In addition to giving thought to the questions or prompts, teachers need to consider the potential value of the answers when conducting data analyses. Student responses, whether correct or incorrect, can reveal quite a bit about student knowledge *if* the possible answers are thoughtfully written.

Figure 6.4   Key Terms for Bloom's Taxonomy Levels

Bloom's Taxonomy	Key Words
Knowledge	define, describe, identify, label, list, match, name
Comprehension	translate, rewrite, summarize, paraphrase
Application	apply, demonstrate, solve, relate, demonstrate, compute
Analysis	analyze, break down, compare, contrast, differentiate, infer, identify
Synthesis	categorize, combine, compile, generate, relate, create
Evaluation	critique, defend, criticize, evaluate, interpret, justify

Earth science teachers and collaborators, John Train and Vivienne Glass, developed a multiple-choice assessment to determine if their students were understanding the minilectures they had each presented during a week studying the issue of global warming. Consider this question from their assessment:

The graph below shows data from the National Oceanic and Atmospheric Administration (NOAA) website (http://www.ncdc.noaa.gov/paleo/globalwarming/what.html). Given an understanding of the current research surrounding global warming, which of the following statements best describes how a NOAA scientist might interpret this data?

a) As CO_2 increased due to human activities from the 1900s to the present, global air temperature increased.

b) As CO_2 increased due to human activities from the 1900s to the present, global air temperature decreased.

c) As lava temperatures increased from the 1900s to the present, CO_2 levels increased.

d) As lava temperatures increased from the 1900s to the present, CO_2 levels decreased.

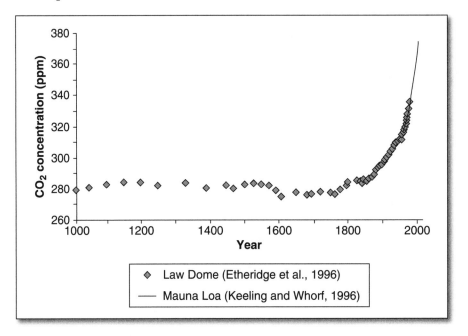

SOURCE: National Climatic Data Center: U.S. Department of Commerce. http://www .ncdc.noaa.gov/paleo/globalwarming/what.html

When Mr. Train and Ms. Glass reviewed the student responses to this question, here's what they found:

- 62% chose "a" (correct answer).
- 18% chose "b."
- 10% chose "c."
- 10% chose "d."

The ensuing conversation between Mr. Train and Ms. Glass revealed a fairly in-depth understanding of what students knew about the relationship between carbon dioxide levels and temperature of the atmosphere.

Ms. Glass began as follows: "Most of the students knew that the graphs indicated that CO_2 was increasing between 1900 and the present. We can see this because 80% of the students answered either "a" or "b." The students that answered "b" knew how to read the graph, but they didn't understand that increased CO_2 in the atmosphere corresponded to global warming. An understanding of this correlation is essential to the issue of global warming. We may need to go back and revisit this idea." Mr. Train added as follows: "I'm concerned about the 20% that answered 'c' and 'd.' We need to review graph interpretation with these students. They clearly did not look at the axes to correctly interpret the meaning of the graph. Also, the students who chose 'd' don't have an understanding that CO_2 levels have increased since the early 1900s. We need to review the concepts behind increased human activities during the 20th century."

Mr. Train and Ms. Glass created an assessment that would allow them to analyze their students' understandings in a very focused manner. This was intentional. Their collaboration involved a great deal of conversation centered around the ultimate goals for learning. For this question in particular, both teachers wanted students to be able to interpret and apply learned information. They wanted their students to go beyond the basic knowledge level of competence. Additionally, the teachers wanted each response to reveal something about what students knew or conversely what they still needed to learn. Occasionally, Mr. Train and Ms. Glass write an assessment item that is misleading or confusing. Usually this is revealed by the student response data. When this happens, they either revise the question or simply throw it out. For the global warming assessment, they only had eight items on their assessment because each question took considerable time to create and analyze in terms of student data. Eight questions were enough to help them determine next steps in terms of instruction.

TYPES OF ASSESSMENTS USEFUL IN SCIENCE

In addition to multiple-choice items, there are a number of ways in which science teachers can use reading and writing to assess student learning. As will be discussed, these alternative ways of checking for understanding provide the teacher with information he or she can use in future instructional planning.

Graphic Organizers

Rooted in the work of Ausubel (1960), graphic organizers have become a staple of many science classrooms. In fact, graphic organizers provide a logical and effective means by which a student's understanding of the relatedness and connectivity of science concepts may be evaluated. According to Klassen (2006), "meaningful learning is characterized by a high degree of integration of existing memory structures (prior knowledge) with new knowledge" (p. 15). This integration is essential if later recall of information is a goal of instruction. As Ausubel, Novak, and Hanesian (1978) noted, the meaningfulness of content is dependent upon how the content relates to prior learning. Additionally, meaningfulness is dependent upon each individual learner's interaction with the material. Graphic organizers provide opportunities for individuals to identify and show what is meaningful to them. Because graphic organizers often represent a person's unique way of integrating information into prior knowledge schema, caution should be used when trying to standardize the evaluation of a graphic organizer.

Graphic organizers as tools for assessment can be developed in several different ways. Teachers can create scaffolding templates that provide places for students to document terms or ideas. To evaluate a deeper understanding of concepts, students might develop their own graphic organizers from scratch—perhaps with a partner. Science topics often lend themselves nicely to a particular format for creating a graphic organizer. For example, *cycles*, like the water cycle, nitrogen cycle, or carbon-oxygen cycle, would be appropriately mapped using a cycle diagram (Figure 6.5). Processes or lab procedures might be depicted using a hierarchical structure. A compare and contrast structure might work for a review of mitosis and meiosis (see Figure 6.6) and a tree diagram might be used to explain the process of collisions (see Figure 6.7).

Performance Assessment

Because today's science reform efforts are aimed at helping students to understand the *nature of science*—a nature built on problems, questions, and inquiry-based experimentation—it is logical for teachers to incorporate performance assessment as a tool to evaluate a student's progress toward inquiry-based thinking. Southerland, Smith, Sowell, and Kittleson (2007) stated the following:

> Teachers are asked to provide learning experiences that actively engage students in learning the substantive content of science through classroom-based inquiry, enabling them to understand the facts, principles, and theories of the discipline as well as the ability to comprehend, interpret, analyze, reason, and communicate about discipline-specific ideas. (p. 60)

When conducting a performance assessment, students are presented with a task that is related to learned concepts yet is still novel in terms of procedures and specific situations. In this way, an understanding of how students approach a problem using the skills of inquiry that characterize the *nature of science* may be evaluated.

Figure 6.5 Graphic Organizer for the Water Cycle

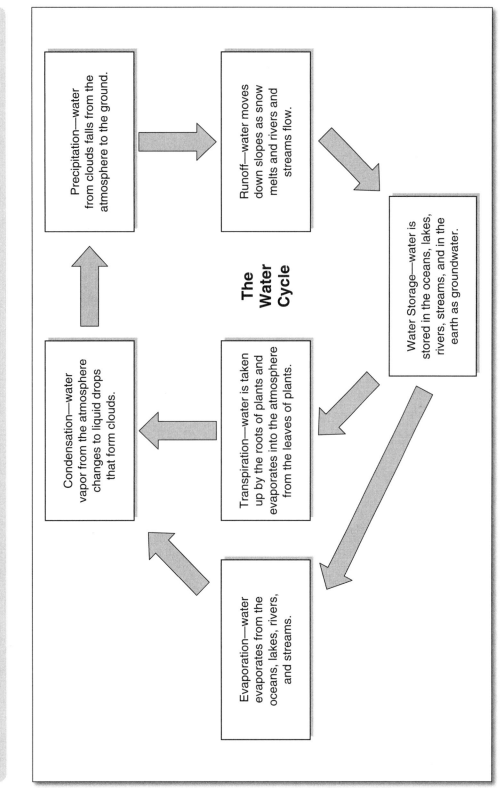

Figure 6.6 Graphic Organizer for Comparing Mitosis and Meiosis

Compare/Contrast	Mitosis	Meiosis
Production of cells	Somatic cells; for growth and repair, two daughter cells	Sex cells, four daughter cells
Nuclear division	One division	Two divisions
Metaphase	Chromosomes line up single-file	Chromosomes line up as homologous pairs
Daughter cells	Two sets of chromosomes each	Only one member of each pair of chromosomes

Figure 6.7 Graphic Organizer for Explaining Collisions

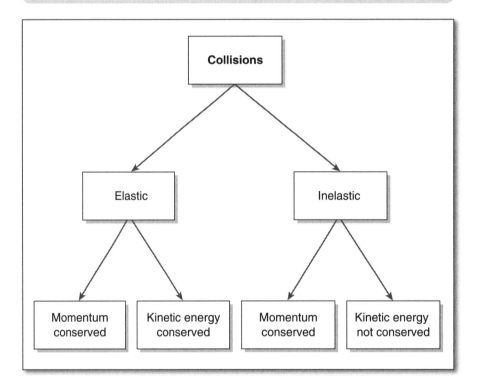

Physics teacher Shirley Roberts asked her students to work in partnerships to create a model of a functioning roller coaster that would incorporate the concepts of kinetic energy, potential energy, momentum, mass, and the law of conservation of energy. The concepts had all been studied

previously but the specific situation, that of a roller coaster, was novel for the students. Partners were provided with an array of materials including plastic tubing, marbles of varying sizes, duct tape, wooden dowels, construction paper, cardboard, metal tubes, and straws. They were also permitted to bring in materials from home. While some students struggled with the development of a structure that would allow a marble to run the full course of the coaster, others had ideas that worked right away. Students learned from mistakes, revised prototypes, and ultimately all met with success. In this particular case, Ms. Roberts' performance assessment allowed for modifications, rethinking, and revision. She wanted to assess her students' understanding of the *nature of science.* In the end, all students successfully showed that they understood the working principles of problem solving in science. As a companion to this assessment, Ms. Roberts presented students with an additional assessment, a more traditional pencil-paper test, to determine if individuals understood the theoretical foundations of potential energy, kinetic energy, and momentum. Clearly, practice and theory each hold weight in science, and performance assessment is a logical way to assess the former.

As with the use of graphic organizers, performance assessment asks students to draw upon their unique ways of connecting and thinking about science ideas. Consequently, teachers need to be tuned into the diverse, distinctive ways that inquiry-based thinking may be approached by individuals in the classroom. This is particularly important when evaluating performance assessments.

FINAL THOUGHTS ABOUT ASSESSMENT

We like to think of assessment as a means to retool, revise, and improve instruction and the resultant learning for students. It is directly connected to meeting the needs of all students in a classroom—a directive of most school districts today. A teacher needs to be constantly aware of whose needs are being met, who needs support, and who needs more challenges. Assessment can range from small-scale efforts, like listening in on a two-minute partner talk, to a full-scale weeklong performance effort. In fact, we advocate the use of a wide array of frequently administered assessments. For any teacher, assessment is a means to understand your students so that you can tailor content delivery to meet their needs.

When interpreting assessment data, collaboration with course-alike colleagues—teachers who teach the same courses, such as Earth science or biology—can help with data analysis. Another pair of eyes looking at a question or prompt might help you to identify areas that need clarification or response choices that need rewriting. Dialogue between teacher peers looking at student data together can help to illuminate meaning and implications for instruction. It is clearly worth the effort it takes to arrange schedules and meeting locations.

Last, remember that assessment needs to be directly tied to instructional goals. Starting with national, state, or district objectives as a foundation for assessment development ensures that course goals are tied to student outcomes. The development of curriculum and instructional strategies can evolve as a result of assessment objectives and data analysis.

Teaching science is about student learning. If educators are to help develop scientifically literate young people who can converse, write, and think about the world around them, we must provide opportunities for students to practice reading, talking, and listening in science classes. Collaborating with colleagues about science and science instruction is not only energizing for the instructors, it is ultimately of great value to the students. Through collaborative efforts, teachers can guide students toward a better understanding of the foundations of our world, including nature, technology, energy, and the interactions between these elements.

References

Albright, L., & Ariail, M. (2005). Tapping the potential of teacher read-alouds in middle schools. *Journal of Adolescent & Adult Literacy, 48,* 582–591.

Ausubel, D. P. (1960). The use of advance organizers in the learning and retention of meaningful verbal material. *Journal of Educational Psychology, 51,* 267–272.

Ausubel, D. P., Novak, J. D., & Hanesian, H. (1978). *Educational psychology: A cognitive view* (2nd ed.). New York: Holt, Rinehart & Winston.

Beck, I. I., McKeown, M. G., & Kucan, I. (2002). *Bringing words to life.* New York: Guilford.

Beck, I. L., McKeown, M. G., & McCaslin, E. S. (1983). All contexts are not created equal. *Elementary School Journal, 83,* 177–181.

Beck, I. L., Perfetti, C., & McKeown, M. (1982). Effects of long-term vocabulary instruction on lexical access and reading comprehension. *Journal of Educational Psychology, 74*(4), 506–521.

Black, P. (1993). Formative and summative assessment by teachers. *Studies in Science Education, 21,* 49–97.

Bloom, B. S. (1956). *Taxonomy of educational objectives: The classification of educational goals: Handbook I, cognitive domain.* New York: Longman.

California Department of Education. (2002). *Standards for investigation and experimentation.* Retrieved May 25, 2009, from http://www.cde.ca.gov/BE/ST/SS/ documents/sciencestnd.pdf

Carlo, M., August, D., McLaughlin, B., Snow, C., Dressler, C., Lippman, D., et al. (2004). Closing the gap: Addressing the vocabulary needs of English-language learners in bilingual and mainstream classrooms. *Reading Research Quarterly, 39*(2), 188–215.

Chaopricha, S. (1997). *Coauthoring as learning and enculturation: A study of writing in biochemistry.* Unpublished doctoral dissertation, University of Wisconsin, Madison.

Cooper. P., & Morreale, S. (2003). *Creating competent communicators: Activities for teaching speaking, listening, and media literacy in grades 7–12.* Scottsdale, AZ: Holcomb Hathaway Publishers.

Coxhead, A. (2000). A new academic word list. *TESOL Quarterly, 34*(2), 213–238.

Csikszentmihalyi, M. (1990). *Flow: The psychology of optimal experience.* New York: Harper & Row.

Csikszentmihalyi, M., & Hermanson, K. (1995). Intrinsic motivation in museums: What makes visitors want to learn? *Museum News, 74,* 34–61.

Csikszentmihalyi, M., & Nakamura, J. (1989). The dynamics of intrinsic motivation: A study of adolescents. In C. Ames & R. Ames (Eds.), *Research in motivation and education* (pp. 73–101). San Diego, CA: Academic Press.

Dodge, B. (2007). *WebQuest.org.* Retrieved May, 2007, from http://webquest.org/index.php

Donahue, D. M. (2000). Experimenting with texts: New science teachers' experience and practice as readers and teachers of reading. *Journal of Adolescent & Adult Literacy, 43,* 728–740.

Firlik, K. (2006). *Another day in the frontal lobe: A brain surgeon exposes life on the inside.* New York: Random House.

Fisher, D., & Frey, N. (2004). *Improving adolescent literacy: Strategies at work.* Upper Saddle River, NJ: Pearson Education.

Fisher, D., & Frey, N. (2007). *Checking for understanding: Formative assessment techniques for your classroom.* Alexandria, VA: Association for Supervision and Curriculum Development.

Fisher, D., & Frey, N. (2008a). *Better learning through structured teaching: A framework for the gradual release of responsibility.* Alexandria, VA: Association for Supervision and Curriculum Development.

Fisher, D., & Frey, N. (2008b). *Word wise and content rich: Five essential steps to teaching academic vocabulary.* Portsmouth, NH: Heinemann.

Fisher, D., & Ivey, G. (2005). Literacy and language as learning in content area classes: A departure from "every teacher a teacher of reading." *Action in Teacher Education, 27*(2), 3–11.

Fitzgerald, J. (1983). Helping readers gain self-control over reading comprehension. *The Reading Teacher, 37,* 249–253.

Frayer, D. A., Frederick, W. D., & Klausmeier, H. J. (1969). *A schema for testing the level of concept mastery* (Working Paper No. 16). Madison: Wisconsin Research and Development Center for Cognitive Learning.

Graves, M. F. (2006). *The vocabulary book: Learning and instruction.* New York: Teachers College Press.

Hand, B. M., & Prain, V. (1996). Writing for learning in science: A model for use within classrooms. *Australian Science Teachers Journal, 42,* 23–27.

Hand, B. M., Lawrence, C., Prain, V., & Yore, L. D. (1999). A writing in science framework designed to enhance science literacy. *International Journal of Science Education, 21,* 1021–1035.

Harmon, J. M., Wood, K. D., Hedrick, W. B., Vintinner, J., & Willeford, T. (2009). Interactive word walls: More than just reading the writing on the walls. *Journal of Adolescent & Adult Literacy, 52,* 398–409.

Heimlich, J. E., & Pittelman, S. D. (1986). *Semantic mapping: Classroom applications.* Newark, DE: International Reading Association.

Hicks, K., & Wadlington, B. (1994, March). *The efficacy of shared reading with teens.* Paper presented at the conference of the Association for Childhood Educational International Study, New Orleans, LA.

Hug, B., Krajcik, J. S., & Marx, R. W. (2005). Using innovative learning technologies to promote learning and engagement in an urban science classroom. *Urban Education, 40,* 446–472.

Ivey, G., & Broaddus, K. (2001). 'Just plain reading': A survey of what makes students want to read in middle school classrooms. *Reading Research Quarterly, 36,* 50–377.

Jenkinson, E. B. (1988). Learning to write/writing to learn. *Phi Delta Kappan, 69,* 712–717.

Kirkman, J. (2005). *Good style: Writing for science and technology.* New York: Routledge.

Klassen, S. (2006). Contextual assessment in science education: Background, issues, and policy. *Science Education, 90,* 820–851.

Kohn, A. (1993). *Punished by rewards: The trouble with gold stars, incentive plans, A's, praise, and other bribes.* New York: Houghton Mifflin.

Kohn, A. (2002, September). Education's rotten apples: From math instruction to state assessments, bad practices can undermine the good. *Education Weekly, 22*(3), 1. Retrieved November 1, 2006, from http://www.edweek.org/ew/ewstory.cfm?slug=03kohn.h22&keywords=Kohn

Lapp, D., & Flood, J. (2005). Exemplary reading instruction in urban elementary schools: How reading develops, how students learn, and teachers teach. In J. Flood & P. Anders (Eds.), *The literacy development of students in urban schools: Research and policy* (pp. 153–179). Newark, DE: International Reading Association.

Manzo, A. V. (1969). ReQuest procedure. *Journal of Reading, 13,* 123–126.

Marzano, R. J. (2004). *Building background knowledge for academic achievement.* Alexandria, VA: Association for Supervision and Curriculum Development.

Medina, J. (2008). *Brain rules: 12 principles for surviving and thriving at work, home, and school.* Seattle, WA: Pear Press.

Moje, E. (2008). Foregrounding the disciplines in secondary literacy teaching and learning: A call for change. *Journal of Adolescent & Adult Literacy, 52*(2), 96–107.

Nagy, W. E., & Anderson, R. C. (1984). How many words are there in printed school English? *Reading Research Quarterly, 19,* 304–330.

Norris, S., & Phillips, L. (2003). How literacy in its fundamental sense is central to scientific literacy. *Science Education, 87,* 224–240.

Ogle, D. (1986). K-W-L: A teaching model that develops active reading of expository text. *The Reading Teacher, 39,* 564–570.

Palincsar, A. S., & Brown, A. L. (1984). Reciprocal teaching of comprehension-fostering and comprehension-monitoring activities. *Cognition and Instruction, 1,* 117–175.

Pearson, P. D., & Gallagher, M. (1983). The instruction of reading comprehension. *Contemporary Educational Psychology, 8,* 317–344.

Pittelman, S. D., Heimlich, J. E., Berglund, R. L., & French, M. P. (1991). *Semantic feature analysis: Classroom applications.* Newark, DE: International Reading Association.

Prain, V., & Hand, B. (1996). Writing for learning in secondary science: Rethinking practices. *Teaching & Teacher Education, 12,* 609–626.

Raphael, T. E. (1982). Teaching children question-answering strategies. *The Reading Teacher, 36,* 186–191.

Raphael, T. E. (1984). Teaching learners about sources of information for answering questions. *Journal of Reading, 27,* 303–311.

Raphael, T. E. (1986). Teaching children question-answering relationships, revisited. *The Reading Teacher, 39,* 516–522.

Ruiz-Primo, M. A., & Furtak, E. M. (2006). Exploring teachers' informal formative assessment practices and students' understanding in the context of scientific inquiry. *Journal of Research in Science Teaching, 44,* 57–84.

Sanders, J., Patrick, J., Dedeoglu, H., Charbonnet, S., Henkel, M., Zhihui, F., et al. (2007). Infusing reading into science learning. *Educational Leadership, 64,* 62–66.

Schneider, R. M., Krajcik, J., Marx, R. W., & Soloway, E. (2002). Performance of students in project-based science classrooms on a national measure of science achievement. *Journal of Research in Science Teaching, 39,* 410–422.

Shanahan, T., & Shanahan, C. (2008). Teaching disciplinary literacy to adolescents: Rethinking content-area literacy. *Harvard Educational Review, 78*(1), 40–59.

Shevick, E. (1998). *Science action labs—Science fun: Activities to encourage students to think and solve problems.* Carthage, IL: Teaching & Learning Company.

Southerland, S. A., Smith, L. K., Sowell, S. P., & Kittleson, J. M. (2007). Resisting unlearning: Understanding science education's response to the United States's National Accountability Movement. *Review of Research in Education, 31,* 45–77.

Stahl, S.A., & Fairbanks, M.M. (1986). The effects of vocabulary instruction: A model-based meta-analysis. *Review of Educational Research, 56*(1), 72–110.

Stahl, S. A. (1999). *Vocabulary development.* Cambridge, MA: Brookline Books.

Stahl, S. A., & Nagy, W. E. (2006). *Teaching word meanings.* Mahwah, NJ: Lawrence Erlbaum.

Stauffer, R. G., & Harrell, M. M. (1975). Individualized reading-thinking activities. *The Reading Teacher, 28,* 765–769.

Stern, L., & Ahlgren, A. (2002). Analysis of students' assessments in middle school curriculum materials: Aiming precisely at benchmarks and standards. *Journal of Research in Science Teaching, 39,* 889–910.

Tocci, S. (2004). *The periodic table.* Winnipeg, Manitoba, Canada: Children's Press.

Trends in International Mathematics and Science Study (TIMMS). (n.d.). Retrieved May 25, 2009, from http://nces.ed.gov/timss/results03_fourth03.asp

Yore, L. D. (2000). Enhancing science literacy for all students with embedded reading instruction and writing-to-learn activities. *Journal of Deaf Studies and Deaf Education, 5,* 105–122.

Yore, L. D., Florence, M. K., Pearson, T., & Weaver, A. (2006). Written discourse in scientific communities: A conversation with two scientists about their views of science, use of language, role of writing in doing science, and compatibility between their epistemic views and language. *International Journal of Science Education, 28*, 109–141.

Yore, L. D., Hand, B. M., & Florence, M. K. (2004). Scientists' views of science, models of writing, and science writing practices. *Journal of Research in Science Teaching, 41*, 338–369.

Yore, L. D., Hand, B., & Prain, V. (1999, January). *Writing to learn science: Breakthroughs, barriers, and promises*. Paper presented at the International Conference of the Association for Educating Teachers in Science, Austin, TX.

Index